# Psychological Tools

# Psychological Tools
## A Sociocultural Approach to Education

## Alex Kozulin

Harvard University Press
Cambridge, Massachusetts
London, England
1998

*Library of Congress Cataloging-in-Publication Data*

Kozulin, Alex.

Psychological tools : a sociocultural approach

to education / Alex

Kozulin.

p. cm.

Includes bibliographical references and index.

ISBN 0-674-72141-1 (alk. paper)

1. Learning, Psychology of. 2. Cognition—Social aspects.

3. Learning—Social aspects. 4. Education psychology.

5. Vygotskiĭ, L. S. (Lev Semenovich), 1896–1934. I. Title.

BF318.K65 1998

153.1′5—dc21 98-23168

# Contents

# Preface

Here is the problem: "A rope is tied around the Earth's equator. Then a ten-meter-long piece is added to it and the rope is pulled evenly so that everywhere the distance between the Earth's surface and the rope is the same. The question is: Would this distance be sufficient for a cat to sneak under the rope?"

I was given this problem by my son while I was driving. My first impulse was to take a piece of paper, draw two concentric circles, and start figuring out the difference between their radiuses, knowing that the difference in their circumferences is ten meters. But because I was driving a car and could not draw or write, my thoughts took a different turn. I started thinking of what would happen if the piece were added and kept in just one location. This would produce a loop five meters high. I then imagined the enormous length of the rope (actually 40,192,200 meters) that was expected to absorb this loop and came to the conclusion that the resultant distance from the surface would be extremely small and insufficient for a cat to sneak under. I gave my answer. My son triumphed. I erred.

Why did I err? I erred because I switched from a scientific approach, which required drawing models and writing formulae, to everyday reasoning, which in this instance led me in the wrong direction. The ability to use the scientific approach (though unrealized) was my strong point, the readiness to switch to everyday reasoning, my weakness.

Much of this book is about the changes in our thinking brought about by the use of "paper and pencil," or symbolic tools and their mental equivalents—psychological tools. On the one hand, symbolic tools such as writing, formulae, signs, and notations of different kinds make us very powerful; on the other, they reshape some of our more natural functions, such as memory and imagination, making them dependent on external symbolic aids. Instead of manipulating "$2\pi(R1 - 2)\pi R2 = 10m; R1 - R2 = 1.6m$" in my mind, I was dependent on their symbolic representation on a piece of paper.

The interdependence between human thinking and symbolic systems was first emphasized by Lev Vygotsky (1896–1934), the Russian psychologist and author of the sociocultural theory of cognition and learning. Initially my interest in Vygotsky focused on theoretical issues. How does his theory differ from those of other influential authors such as Piaget? Which aspects of his work were further developed by his followers in the Soviet Union and which became apparent only when Vygotsky's ideas became recognized in the West? What is so special in Vygotsky's theory that makes it attractive and relevant more than half a century after its conception? How can one extend the notion of psychological tools to include, for example, literary texts?

My interest in historical and theoretical issues became complemented by a concern with the more practical educational applications of Vygotsky's ideas. Two factors contributed to this change of focus. One of them was my entrance into the field of cognitive education via the Israeli psychologist and educator Reuven Feuerstein's theory of the mediated learning experience and its applied system of Instrumental Enrichment. The second was my experience of working with new immigrant students from Ethiopia, who had to master all the symbolic tools unknown to them. I had to identify those cognitive gaps that hindered the immigrants' success in the classroom, and then select or design educational interventions that promoted the necessary cognitive change. In the process of doing this—and in agreement with sociocultural theory—many of the cognitive functions that had earlier appeared "natural" revealed their origin in specific educational or experiential practices.

As a result, sociocultural theory appears in this book both as a powerful theoretical paradigm and as a basis for educational applications. The concept of psychological tools finds one of its embodiments in the Instrumental Enrichment cognitive education program. Vygotsky's emphasis on the sociocultural nature of learning and instruction finds its practical equivalent in a study of problem solving in new immigrant students. The distinction between everyday and "scientific" concepts becomes related to contemporary efforts to place conceptual change at the center of the instructional process. If in the problem with which I started this preface we had to go from empirical facts to conceptual knowledge, the chapters that follow will proceed in the opposite direction—from sociocultural theory to its empirical consequences.

# Psychological Tools

# Introduction

This book examines the role of psychological tools in human cognitive development and learning. The concept of psychological tools is one of the cornerstones of the psychological theory of Lev Semyonovich Vygotsky (1896–1934). But in spite of the early appearance of this concept in Vygotsky's writings, the psychological tools paradigm has only recently been recognized in the West, and the applied programs based on it are still in a nascent stage.

Psychological tools are those symbolic artifacts—signs, symbols, texts, formulae, graphic-symbolic devices—that help individuals master their own "natural" psychological functions of perception, memory, attention, and so on. Psychological tools serve as a bridge between individual acts of cognition and the symbolic sociocultural prerequisites of these acts. The concept of psychological tools offers a fresh perspective in the study of comparative cognitive development, classroom learning, cross-cultural differences in cognition, and the possible ways of making education more attuned to the needs of teaching thinking and creative problem-solving.

Chapter 1 provides the historical and theoretical context necessary for understanding Vygotsky's psychological theory in general and the concept of psychological tools in particular. A distinctive feature of Vygotsky's theory is its strong emphasis on the sociocultural character of human cognition. According to Vygotsky, there are two major classes of psychological functions—"natural" and "cultural." One can observe a "natural" dynamic in the unfolding of the child's cognitive functions in

2 ☙ *Psychological Tools*

the course of development and maturation. Human civilization, however, brings about a radical change in this course, by transforming these "natural" functions into "cultural" ones. This change occurs under the influence of material and symbolic tools as well as through different forms of interpersonal communication developed in human society. As a result human beings become endowed with the ability to regulate their "natural" psychological functions by external, and later internalized, symbolic tools. Such an approach to human cognition opens a number of new perspectives. One of them is the investigation of historical and cultural differences in human cognition dependent on the available systems of psychological tools.

This line of study was opened by Vygotsky and Alexander Luria in the early 1930s, to be continued, after a lengthy interruption, by Michael Cole in the United States and Peter Tulviste in Estonia. Others have investigated those activities that foster the use of psychological tools for the modification and control of psychological functions. A special role is played by language, which appears simultaneously as one of the most basic of psychological tools and as a psychological function undergoing change under the influence of literacy and other more complex forms of symbolization. A growing number of scholars, including James Wertsch, Laura Berk, and Rafael Diaz, are pursuing this direction of study.

Finally, there is the important question of the specialized learning activity essential in formal education that can be distinguished from learning in a generic sense. On a theoretical plane this distinction sets the stage for the interrelationship between "natural" development and education. In the applied field it spells out requirements for the organization of learning activities at school that are different from those available in everyday life. Originally developed by Vygotskian followers in the Soviet Union such as Daniel Elkonin and Vasili Davydov, this innovative trend is now attracting considerable attention elsewhere, providing a fresh perspective on such topics as "constructivism" in children's learning and the role of cognitive education in school curriculum.

In Chapter 2 it is argued that a comparison of Vygotsky's and Piaget's views on cognitive development, education, and learning helps to untangle a number of complicated issues that still beset contemporary educational psychology. Vygotsky's and Piaget's systems have a number of common points. Among them is the emphasis on the self-important character of children's thought, which is not a scaled-down version of adult thinking but a unique phenomenon with its own logic, dynamic, and salient features. In addition, in both Vygotskian and Piagetian systems learning is perceived in terms of a transition from action to thought. The roots of inner cognitive schemata are sought in the actual interactive activity of children. Finally, both of these thinkers emphasized the systemic organization of the child's developing thought and the need to understand it as a system rather than as an aggregate of separate abilities, skills, and units of information.

The central difference between the Piagetian and Vygotskian approaches lies in their respective interpretation of who is the active subject of the learning process. For Piaget it is an individual child, who, through active interaction with the physical and social environment, enhances his or her own cognitive schemata. For Vygotsky the learning process has a sociocultural character from its very beginning. The true subject of learning is an integrative whole that includes the child, the adult, and the symbolic tool provided by a given society. If in the Piagetian system the child is presupposed as a true agent of his or her own learning, in the Vygotskian system the child becomes such an independent agent toward the very end of the formal learning experience. These two opposite approaches have found their realization in classroom practice. In American classrooms a rather unexpected blend of the Piagetian system and the principles of progressive education has led to the explosive growth of learning by discovery programs. In the Soviet Union and post-Communist Russia, systematic attempts have been made at developing theoretical learning programs based on the distinction between "scientific" and "spontaneous" concept formation.

Chapter 3 examines the relationship between psychological tools and the principles of mediated learning. According to Vygotsky, there are three major classes of mediating agents: material tools, psychological tools, and the human mediator. Material tools have only an indirect influence on human psychological processes, because they are directed at processes in nature. Material tools do not exist as individual implements; they presuppose collective use, interpersonal communication, and symbolic representation. All these aspects of material tool use influence human cognition, and for this reason sociocultural psychology cannot ignore this class of mediators. Still, symbolic psychological tools play a more important role because they occupy a strategic position "between" stimuli of the world and the inner psychological processes of an individual. Psychological tools thus transform the unmediated interaction of the human being with the world into mediated interaction. Such "natural" psychological functions as perception, memory, and attention become transformed under the influence of psychological tools, generating new cultural forms of psychological functions. The type of these transformations depends on the type of symbolic tools available in a given culture and the conditions under which the appropriation of these tools by individuals is taking place. In the Vygotskian research tradition major emphasis was placed on the type of symbolic tools and their availability. The role of the human mediator was often reduced to that of the mere provider of symbolic tools to the child.

A more comprehensive picture of this process can be obtained if one takes into account the role of the human mediator. Specific parameters of human mediation in learning situations have been elaborated by the Israeli psychologist and educator Reuven Feuerstein in his studies of the mediated learning experience (MLE). The presence of MLE seems to constitute a crucial factor in rendering a child capable of independent learning. More specifically, the presence of MLE creates conditions necessary for the appropriation of psychological tools. Reduced amounts of MLE seriously undermine the child's learning capacity. Specific examples of disabilities and disabling sociocultural conditions leading to an insufficient MLE are discussed. The notion of MLE helps to distinguish between the manifest level of a student's performance and learning potential, which reveals itself under conditions of MLE stimulation. The notion of learning potential is compared to the Vygotskian notion of the zone of proximal development. Both of these theoretical constructs lead to specific cognitive assessment techniques developed by, among others, Ann Brown and Joseph Campione in the United States, Jürgen Guthke in Germany, and Reuven Feuerstein in Israel.

Chapter 4 outlines the current situation in the field of cognitive education and explores the relationships between the psychological tools paradigm and the goals of cognitive intervention. The effects of psychological tools on the learner's cognition can be observed under two conditions: quasi-natural and artificial. Quasi-natural conditions include the acquisition of literacy, numeracy, and other symbolic systems by children in the course of their "normal" development and education. Under these conditions the acquisition of psychological tools is closely intertwined with the acquisition of content material. Not only learners but also educators often cannot distinguish the specific contribution made by psychological tools. This specific contribution becomes apparent under artificial conditions, usually associated with the need to introduce symbolic tools in the form of a specially designed program for children who, because of their cultural difference or peculiar educational history, have been deprived of them. Feuerstein's Instrumental Enrichment (IE) cognitive education program offers a complete system of psychological tools. Originally the IE program was developed for the remediation and enhancement of learning skills of culturally different and educationally deprived adolescents. What makes IE an ideal psychological tools program is its systemic organization, rich assortment of symbolic tools, and emphasis on learning activities congenial to the task of internalizing psychological tools. MLE-based teaching techniques provide a proper vehicle for delivering the IE program to students in need. Specific applications of IE programs with different populations of students are discussed.

Chapter 5 focuses on the cognitive and learning factors that often impede the educational progress of immigrant and minority students. The issue of cross-cultural differences in cognition has both scientific and applied importance. As a scientific problem it poses an important question of the cultural specificity of different types of human cognition; as an applied problem it confronts many educators who work with immigrant or minority students. Three perspectives in the interpretation of cross-cultural differences are discussed: the psychometric perspective (represented by Richard Herrnstein and Charles Murray), which emphasizes the uniformity of human cognition and its ethnically uneven distribution; the sociocultural perspective, which emphasizes the role of culture in either the formation or the realization of cognitive functions (as represented by Alexander Luria and Michael Cole); and the mediated learning experience perspective of Reuven Feuerstein, which emphasizes the role of the human mediator in the development of specific cognitive functions. It is argued that only a combination of sociocultural and mediated learning perspectives on cross-cultural differences in cognition allows one to attain the position that not only leads to a better understanding of minority students' problems but also suggests intervention strategies. Specific difficulties experienced by minority students in the acquisition of school material and academic skills are discussed using data on the educational integration of Ethiopian immigrants to Israel. A special argument is developed against the simplistic dichotomy of un-schooled versus schooled populations. This argument is supported by the case of educated immigrant adults who in spite of their previous formal education demonstrated serious difficulties with Western-type problem-solving skills. The effectiveness of an Instrumental Enrichment cognitive intervention program based on teaching psychological tools to immigrant and minority students is discussed.

Chapter 6 extends the Vygotskian concept of psychological tools to include such supertools as a complex text, for example, a novel. Such an extension allows us to speak about a literary model for psychology. The proposal for this model will be underscored by the discussion of the differences between traditional scientific methodology and the method-ology derived from the humanities. As an illustration I will discuss the contradictory nature of psychoanalytic theory and practice that aspire to appear scientific but in reality employ interpretive techniques similar to those of the humanities.

Literature can serve as a prototype of the most advanced forms of human psychological life and as a concrete psychological tool that me-diates human experiences. The first role of literature is explored by analyzing similarities and differences between the author/hero relation-ships in literature and self/other relationships in real life. The theoretical basis for this discussion is Bakhtin's theory of "authoring." The phe-nomenon of "life as authoring" is discussed as a literary device and as an actual position of the author in modern society. The role of literature as an actual psychological tool is considered in conjunction with the notion of autonomous text (Olson) and its role in the cognitive development of the child. It will be argued that scientific text offers a poor paradigm for an autonomous text, and that intertextually rich humanistic texts are more suitable for this role. The role of classical literary and scientific texts as the basis for more cognitively oriented education is discussed.

Chapter 7 presents an argument in favor of prospective, rather than retrospective, education. The changing roles of teachers, students, and learning material are discussed and the possible contribution of sociocultural theory is outlined. Traditional education is essentially ret-rospective, because it teaches students how to reproduce already known answers to previously posed questions and how to use skills that have proved to be useful in the past. Under the dynamic conditions of mod-ernity, the necessity of prospective education becomes obvious. Prospective education implies that students should be capable of approaching problems that do not exist at the moment of their learning. To achieve this capability, students should be oriented toward productive rather than reproductive knowledge. Productive knowledge requires a radical shift from acquiring information to cognitive education. At the lower stages of this process the acquisition of basic psychological tools and their proper mediation is essential. At the higher stages the acquisition of the more complex "languages" of science, computers, philosophy, and literary discourse become most important. The term "language" is used here not as a metaphor, but as a practical direction toward teaching these subjects as "languages" and symbolic tools rather than as bodies of information.

# 1 🐟

# The Concept of Psychological Activity

The concept of psychological activity is central to Vygotskian psychology. Its importance can be compared to that of the concept of behavior in American psychology and the concept of consciousness in classical European psychology of the nineteenth century. The concept of activity permeates the work of all Vygotsky's followers both in Russia and in the West, but exactly for that reason it has been difficult to define it clearly. Since the time of its inception in the 1920s, this category has undergone a metamorphosis and has been the subject of so many disputes that it cannot be adequately comprehended outside the context of its history.

The goal of this chapter is to provide a historical-theoretical analysis of the evolution of the concept of activity in Vygotskian psychology. The origin of this concept can be found in the early writings of Vygotsky (1979, 1994), who suggested that socially meaningful activity *(Tatigkeit)* may serve as an explanatory principle in regard to, and be considered as a generator of, human consciousness. The concept of activity was then incorporated by Vygotsky in his cultural-historical theory of higher mental functions and used in conjunction with his studies of language development and concept formation.

There seem to be two dramatic events in the history of the concept of activity. The first occurred in the mid-1930s, when a group of Vygotsky's disciples split from their teacher and came up with a "revisionist" version of the concept. This "revisionist" theory put practical (material) activity at the forefront while simultaneously playing down the role of symbolic tools as mediators of human activity (Leontiev and Luria, 1956;

Zinchenko, 1984). This version of the activity theory was elaborated by Leontiev (1978, 1981), who gained in the Soviet Union the status of official interpreter of Vygotsky's ideas. Thus the myth of direct continuity between Vygotsky's and Leontiev's theories was born. Only since the late 1970s has this myth been subjected to critical scrutiny. The late 1970s also saw the second dramatic event in the history of Vygotsky's ideas. After a delay of nearly half a century Western psychology finally "discovered" Vygotsky, and his writings became available to English-speaking readers (Vygotsky, 1978, 1986, 1987; Vygotsky and Luria, 1993; Van der Veer and Valsiner, 1994; Wertsch, 1981). Vygotsky's ideas became used with increasing frequency in developmental and educational psychology, psycholinguistics, and in a new field designated as sociocultural studies (Wertsch, 1985; Moll, 1990; Forman, Minick, and Addison Stone, 1993). In all these diverse applications the notion of psychological activity appeared again and again as a problem that should be confronted both theoretically and practically.

## Activity as an Explanatory Principle

The problem of activity emerged for the first time in Vygotsky's (1979) paper "Consciousness as a Problem of Psychology of Behavior," published in 1925. In this article Vygotsky sought to restore the legitimacy of the concept of consciousness, which at that time was aggressively challenged by behaviorists in the West and by Pavlovians in the Soviet Union. Yet though he returned consciousness to its proper place within psychology, Vygotsky was not ready to return to the traditional introspective mentalistic psychology of the nineteenth century. Vygotsky's major objection to the mentalistic tradition was that it confined itself to a vicious circle of theorizing in which states of consciousness are explained through the concept of consciousness. Behaviorism, in its denial of consciousness, simply avoided the problem by declaring that all psychological phenomena are merely derivatives of reflex-like behavior.

In his attempt to bring consciousness back to psychology, Vygotsky discovered a number of human activities capable of serving as *generators* of consciousness. He points first of all to the historical nature of human experience. Human beings make a wide use of nonbiological heredity-transmitting knowledge, experiences, and symbolic tools from generation to generation. An individual lives not so much in the world of his or her experience as in a world perched at the top of all of previous history. The second aspect of human experience is its indebtedness to the social environment and the experiences of others. I-Other relationships play a central role in Vygotsky's theoretical schema. An individual becomes aware of him- or herself only in and through interactions with others.

> The mechanism of social behavior and the mechanism of consciousness are the same . . . We are aware of ourselves, for we are aware of others, and in the same way as we know others; and this is as it is because we in relations to ourselves are in the same [position] as others are to us . . . I am aware of myself only to the extent that I am another for myself, i.e. only to the extent that I can perceive anew my own responses as new stimuli. (Vygotsky, 1979, pp. 29–30)

There is a striking similarity between this statement and the concept of the significant symbol that the American psychologist George H. Mead developed at about the same time:

> As we shall see, the same procedure which is responsible for the genesis and existence of mind or consciousness—namely the taking of the attitude of the other toward one's self, or toward one's own behavior—also necessarily involves the genesis and existence at the same time of significant symbols, or significant gestures . . . Gestures become significant symbols when they implicitly arouse in the individual making them the same responses which they explicitly arouse, or are supposed to arouse, in other individuals, the individuals to whom they are addressed. (Mead, 1974, pp. 47–48; see also Valsiner and Van der Veer, 1988)

The last characteristic feature of human experience is its "double nature," by which Vygotsky meant the existence of mental images and schemas prior to actual action. Human experience is always present in two different planes—the plane of actual occurrences and the plane of their internal cognitive schematizations. As we will see later, language and other symbolic artifacts play a central role in creating this "duality" of human experience.

In his article Vygotsky (1979) suggested a number of hypotheses concerning the process of generating human consciousness "from outside." Only a few of these ideas survived in his later works. His major achievement, however, was in making a theoretical demarcation between the "subject of study" and the "explanatory principle" (see Davydov and Radzikhovsky, 1985; Kozulin, 1990a). If consciousness is to become a subject of psychological study, it cannot simultaneously serve as an explanatory principle. Thus another candidate for the role of the explanatory principle should be found. Vygotsky suggested that sociocultural activity serves as such an explanatory source. He thus broke the vicious circle within which the phenomena of consciousness used to be explained through the concept of consciousness, and similarly behavior through the concept of behavior, and established premises for a unified theory of behavior and mind on the basis of sociocultural activity.

## Theoretical Background

To understand the theoretical background against which activity emerged as an explanatory principle, we must look into the intricate circumstances that characterized the Soviet psychological scene in the 1920s. The appearance of Soviet psychology in that period is quite misleading. It seemed to be almost completely dominated by the reflexological approach, peppered by random and often quite meaningless quotations from Marx, Engels, and Lenin. This surface structure was rather thin, however, covering much more complex and creative strata of psychological thought (Kozulin, 1984).

In reality Russian psychology, both before and after the Revolution, was deeply dependent on the European psychological tradition. Even at the reflexological approach's peak of popularity, practitioners remained committed to a much wider understanding of human behavior and mind. There was no equivalent of the American "age of behaviorism" in the Soviet Union. Although committed to the new "Marxist psychology," Soviet psychologists of the 1920s did not forget classical figures of European psychology such as Wilhelm Wundt. What is important is that Wundt was known in the Soviet Union not only as a champion of the introspectionist method, but also as a pioneer of cultural psychology *(Volkerpsychologie)* (Wundt, 1920). The French psychological school of Pierre Janet had a number of followers in Russia (and later in the Soviet Union) and left a lasting impression on Vygotsky. Vygotsky often quoted Janet's statement that a psychological function appears twice in the life of the individual: first as an interpersonal function and than as intrapersonal function (see Van der Veer and Valsiner, 1988). In the social sciences Marxism, though dominant, was hardly the only source of ideas regarding the relationship between social forces and individual mind. The works of the French sociological school of Émile Durkheim and the anthropological approach of Lucien Lévy-Bruhl were seriously studied by Vygotsky and his colleagues, who found the notion of "collective representations" quite useful for their sociocultural approach to the human mind (see Van der Veer and Valsiner, 1991). The holistic approach of Gestalt psychology and Kurt Lewin also found a receptive audience. Kurt Koffka later traveled to Soviet Central Asia in order to participate in the Vygotsky-Luria expedition that studied cognitive functions of the members of "traditional" preliterate society (Harrower, 1984). Finally, Vygotsky and his colleagues became some of the early enthusiastic readers of works published by young Jean Piaget. In 1932 Piaget's first two books were published in Russian with Vygotsky's introduction.

In the Soviet Union itself the 1920s were characterized not only by the dominance of Marxism but also by the explosive development of other modernist theories, especially in the fields of linguistics and literary theory. These theories brought revolutionary changes in our understanding of the place of different speech genres in everyday and literary "texts." They also put forward the issue of the dialogicality of human experience. Some of these ideas later found their place in Vygotsky's sociocultural study of the relationship between language and thought (Kozulin, 1990a; Wertsch, 1991).

The dominant Marxist orientation itself was quite congenial to Vygotsky's emphasis on activity. In order to appreciate the influence of Marxism one must be able, however, to distinguish between the hodgepodge of Marxist quotations characteristic of the works produced by certain groups of new Soviet psychologists, and the thoughtful use of Hegelian and Marxist theories made by Vygotsky. First of all, Vygotsky decisively rejected Marxism as a dogmatic ideological yardstick and ridiculed attempts to create a new psychology by concocting a number of "dialectical" and "materialistic" passages. His criticism was harsh and his verdict rigorous: Vygotsky claimed that his opponents sought Marxist support "in the wrong places," that they assimilated "the wrong material," and that they used the available texts "in a wrong way" (Vygotsky, 1982, p. 397).

What Vygotsky sought and found in Marx was a social theory of human activity *(Tatigkeit)* set in opposition to naturalism and the passive receptivity of the empiricist tradition. Marx attracted Vygotsky with his concept of human praxis, that is, concrete historical activity that serves as a generator of different forms of human consciousness. From Hegel, Vygotsky also took a historical attitude toward the analysis of forms and stages in the development of human consciousness. This historically concrete human praxis that accounts for the special social and historical character of human existence and experience became a prototype for the concept of activity as an explanatory principle in psychology (Kozulin, 1990a, chap. 3).

According to Vygotsky, human behavior and mind should be considered in terms of purposive and culturally meaningful actions rather than in terms of adaptive biological reactions. Objects of human experience, and therefore objects of psychological experimentation, should be things, processes, and events that are culturally meaningful, and not just abstract stimuli. Activity then takes the place of hyphen in the formula S-R (stimulus-response), turning it into the formula subject-activity-object, where both subject and object are historically and socially specific.

## The Sociocultural Theory of Higher Mental Functions

According to Vygotsky, the actualization of human activity requires such intermediaries as symbolic psychological tools and the means of interpersonal communication. The concept of the psychological tool arose first by analogy with the material tool that serves as a mediator between the human hand and the object of action. The change in material tools has a reciprocal effect on the entire life of the individual: "The entire existence of an Australian aborigine depends on his boomeranging, just as the entire existence of modern England depends upon her machines. Take the boomerang away from the aborigine, make him a farmer, then out of necessity he will have to completely change his life style, his habits, his entire way of thinking, his entire nature" (Vygotsky and Luria, 1993, p. 74).

Like material tools, psychological tools are artificial formations. By their nature, both are social. However, whereas material tools are aimed at the control of processes in nature, psychological tools master the natural behavioral and cognitive processes of the individual. Unlike material tools, which serve as conductors of human activity aimed at external objects, psychological tools are internally oriented, transforming the inner, natural psychological processes into higher mental functions. In their external form psychological tools are symbolic artifacts such as signs, symbols, languages, formulae, and graphic devices. For example, if an elementary, natural memorizing effort directly connects event A with event B, then a higher function of memory replaces this direct connection by two others: A to X and X to B, where X is an artificial psychological tool, such as a knot on a string, a written note, or a mnemonic scheme. This transition from natural to cultural functions occurs both historically and in individual development. Historically one can observe how the simple use of naturally existent signs, such as tracks, is replaced by the artificial creation of signs for the purpose of memorization:

> From the ability to find paths, that is, from the ability to use tracks as signs that reveal and remind him the whole complex pictures—from the use of a sign—a "primitive" man, at a certain stage of his development, arrives for the first time at the creation of an artificial sign . . . Writing in its initial form appears on the scene precisely as such an auxiliary means, with the help of which man begins to control his memory. Our written word has a very long history. The first tools of memory are signs, as, for example [the] golden figures of West African storytellers; each figure recalls some particular tale. Each of such figures seems to represent the initial name of a long story—for example the moon. Essentially, the bag with such figures represents a primitive table of contents for such a storyteller. (Vygotsky and Luria, 1993, p. 101)

Vygotsky thus made a principal distinction between the "lower," natural mental processes of perception, attention, memory, and will, and the "higher" or cultural psychological functions that appear under the influence of symbolic tools. The lower functions do not disappear but become superseded and incorporated into the cultural ones. "The memory of man, who knows how to write down what he needs to remember, is trained and consequently develops in a different direction than the memory of a man who is absolutely unable to use signs. Inner development and perfection of memory thus are no longer an independent process, but are dependent on, subordinated to, and defined in the course of these changes originating from outside—from the man's social environment" (Vygotsky and Luria, 1993, p. 105).

If one breaks down a higher mental function into its constituent parts, one finds nothing but natural processes that can be studied in a strict scientific way. One needs no speculative metaphysical principles in order to study these processes. All the building blocks of higher mental functions are absolutely materialistic and can be apprehended by ordinary empirical methods. The latter assumption does not imply, however, that the higher mental functions can be reduced to the natural ones. Decomposition shows us only the material of the higher functions but says nothing about their construction.

The constructive principle of the higher mental functions lies outside the individual—in psychological tools and interpersonal relations. "In the instrumental act, humans master themselves from the outside—through psychological tools" (Vygotsky, 1981, p. 141). Concerning the structural role of interpersonal relations, Vygotsky followed Janet's thesis that interpersonal relations serve as prototypes for intrapersonal processes. The functions first appear as actual interaction between individuals, and then become internalized as intrapsychological functions.

The acknowledgment of the central role of symbolic tools as mediators changed the entire nomenclature of psychological functions. Vygotsky suggested that external forms of activity should be included into the taxonomy of psychological processes together with the cultural forms of such traditionally recognized processes as perception, attention, or memory.

> The logical consequence of the recognition of the primary importance of the use of signs in the history of the development of higher psychological functions, is the inclusion of external symbolic forms of activity (speech, reading, writing, counting and drawing) into the system of psychological categories. They were usually regarded as foreign and additional in relation to the inner psychological processes, but from the new point of view we defend [their right] to be included into the system of higher psychological functions on an equal footing with all other higher psychological processes. We are inclined to regard them, first of all, as particular forms of behavior, shaping themselves

in the course of the social-cultural development of the child and forming an external line in the development of symbolic activity along with the inner line, represented by the cultural development of such functions as practical intellect, perception, memory, etc. (Vygotsky and Luria, 1994, pp. 136–137)

Vygotsky's research program included studies of the transition from the natural to the cultural psychological functions of memory, perception, attention, will, counting, and speech. These studies were conducted in three directions: instrumental, developmental, and cultural-historical. The instrumental aspect included the analysis of changes occurring in psychological functions as a consequence of the introduction of new symbolic mediators or the removal of mediators that had become an integral element of individual activity (Vygotsky, 1981).

The developmental or genetical (from genesis) orientation of Vygotsky's work meant much more than a mere analysis of the unfolding of psychological functions in ontogenesis. Indeed, the very idea of development as an unfolding or a maturation was alien to him. Vygotsky perceived psychological development as a process full of upheavals, crises, and structural changes. The developmental process can be observed in both micro- and macrogenetic perspectives. Microgenetically it reveals itself in the restructuring of the child's thinking and behavior under the influence of a new psychological tool. Macrogenetically development manifests itself as the life-long process of the formation of a system of psychological functions corresponding to the entire system of symbolic means available in a given culture. Education is considered to be an integral element of this macrogenetic process. Rather than a superstructure built on the foundation of psychological functions, educational activity is seen as a process radically changing these very functions (Vygotsky, 1978).

From the general premise of Vygotsky's theory that psychological functions originate in human sociocultural activity, it naturally follows that the types of activity characteristic of different historical epochs and different cultures should be put in correspondence with various forms of memorization, reasoning, problem solving, and so on. There are two major avenues for such an analysis. The first of them relies on historical records and documents and attempts to reconstruct historically distant forms of intelligence on the basis of these records. The second avenue is cross-cultural. By comparing different contemporary cultures and by making certain approximations from some of them and the cultures of the past, one may arrive at conclusions regarding the historical change in human cognition (Vygotsky and Luria, 1993). The most obvious contrast here is between people of preliterate, traditional societies, who rely on a relatively limited number of symbolic tools, and people of industrially developed societies, who, through the system of formal education, become exposed to a wide array of symbolic tools that not only become indispensable as cognitive tools but to a certain extent form the very "reality" of the modern individual. In order to explore this cultural-historical hypothesis Luria undertook a field study in the rural areas of Soviet Central Asia in the early 1930s. Luria's expedition collected rich empirical material about the relationships between literacy, schooling, and involvement in the more modern forms of labor, on the one hand, and the development of specific cognitive functions, on the other (Luria, 1976). This pioneering study of Luria later stimulated a whole series of cross-cultural studies conducted by Cole and his colleagues in Africa and elsewhere (for example, Cole and Scribner, 1974).

## Thought and Language

Although Vygotsky's theory embraced all higher mental functions, Vygotsky himself was primarily interested in the relationship between language and thought. This special interest encompassed a number of related topics, such as the role of speech and writing as psychological tools, different forms of the child's concept formation, the development of universal word meanings and personal senses of a word, the problem of egocentric and inner speech, and others. These studies were collected in a 1934 book *Myshlenie i Rech* (1986), which remains the most popular of Vygotsky's writings. (The work has been published as *Thought and Language* (1986); a literal translation would be *Thinking and Speech*. On translation difficulties, see Kozulin 1990b.)

The development of the "tool" metaphor led Vygotsky to the hypothesis that the structural properties of language must leave their imprint on the entire activity of the child, and that the child's experience itself gradually acquires a symbolic, quasi-linguistic structure. Bringing together such seemingly disparate phenomena as gesture, symbolic play, and children's drawings and scribbles, Vygotsky attempted to show that they represent steps toward the mastery of the symbolic function, which reaches its most revealing form in written speech.

Following Wundt's analysis of human gestures, Vygotsky drew parallels between gestures, primitive pictography, and children's drawings. According to Vygotsky the drawings of younger children serve as the fixation of gesture rather than as the reflection of visual properties of objects. Gesture provides a link connecting pictography with symbolic play.

> For children some objects can readily denote others, replacing them and becoming signs for them, and the degree of similarity between a plaything and the object it denotes is unimportant. What is most important is the utilization of the plaything and the possibility of executing a representational gesture with it. This is the key to the entire symbolic function of child's play . . .
>
> From this point of view, therefore, children's symbolic play can be understood as a very complex system of "speech" through gestures that communicate and indicate the meaning of playthings. (Vygotsky, 1978, p. 108)

In the course of play, the plaything absorbs the meaning of the signified object and then carries it without the assigning gesture. Thus the child first uses a special gesture to designate a broom as a "horse," and next the broom is used in its capacity of a horse without any special gesture. Then the children "discover" that certain properties of playthings fit their roles. For example, when a researcher put down a book with a dark cover and suggested to the child that this would be a forest, the child spontaneously added, "Yes, it's a forest because it's black and dark" (Vygotsky, 1978, p. 109). In this way the child came to the intuitive use of metonymy. Through symbolic play the child mastered symbolic relationships and the conventional character of the relations between signifier and signified. This conventionality is one of the fundamental prerequisites of writing.

Reading and writing appear in Vygotsky's system as special cases of symbolization. Such an understanding guides his educational approach, which puts major emphasis on the child's acquisition of the function of arbitrary symbolization in its various forms. Vygotsky recommended beginning writing instruction by asking children to designate certain objects by pictograms or signs. Once this core symbolic function is acquired, the shift should be made from first-order symbolism, using signs to depict the content of a sentence, to second-order symbolism, using letters to depict words. Some of Vygotsky's insights are incorporated in contemporary reading programs that emphasize the need to teach the function of symbolization prior to engaging children in the specific techniques of writing and spelling (McLane, 1990). The concept of activity thus appears as the actualization of cultural forms of behavior embodied in the use of assigning gestures, symbolic play, and a writing system.

Another aspect of Vygotsky's inquiry into the problem of thought and language concerns concept formation in children. The starting point here was Vygotsky's dissatisfaction with the then existent methods of study, which focused either on verbal definition of some concept or on nonverbal identification of a common feature in a number of objects. The first method, in Vygotsky's opinion, merely elicited ready-made definitions that characterized the child's verbal knowledge rather than concept formation. The second method, based on the function of simple abstraction, disregarded symbolic function, which in Vygotsky's opinion constituted the core of concept formation. To overcome this methodological difficulty Vygotsky suggested the method of so-called double stimulation.

The method of "double stimulation" was developed by Vygotsky's collaborator, Leonid Sakharov (1994), on the basis of the earlier work of the German psychologist Narciss Ach. In this test the child receives a number of objects differing in size, shape, and color and is asked to sort them. Unlike other sorting tests, each object in this test is also coded by a triplet of letters. The child thus can use both the objective characteristics of objects and their coded "names" as bases for classification. In Vygotsky's opinion this constitutes an experimental approximation of the concept formation processes occurring in real life, where children form concepts by combining an analysis of objects' characteristics with verbal definitions provided by adults. Using the method of double stimulation Vygotsky and his colleagues were able to identify a number of stages in the child's concept formation from unorganized congeries to logical concepts (Vygotsky, 1986). Vygotsky's study of concept formation was among the first noticed in the West. Hanfmann and Kasanin (1942) used the method of double stimulation in their study of thinking in schizophrenic patients, while Werner and E. Kaplan (1950) further elaborated some of Vygotsky's ideas in their study of how children assign meanings to meaningless words.

Another colleague of Vygotsky, Jozephina Shif (1935), extended the study of concept formation into an educational setting. Vygotsky (1986) distinguished two types of active experience, which in his opinion led to two different, albeit interrelated, types of concept formation. The first one is a systematically organized experience of formal schooling. This activity, at least in its ideal form, leads to the formation of academic, "scientific" concepts. Scientific concepts are systemically and hierarchically organized, reflect the cultural models of thinking embodied in the natural and social sciences, and are consciously appropriated and used by students. The second type of experience leading to concept formation is the everyday experience of children. This experience is empirically very rich, but it is unsystematic and often unconscious. Everyday experience leads to spontaneous, everyday concepts that can be quite adequate in specific everyday contexts, but are misleading when applied to tasks that require logical, scientific conceptualization.

Vygotsky argued that scientific concepts are not assimilated by the child in a ready-made form, but undergo a process of substantial development. This process depends on the interaction between scientific concepts offered to the child and the child's own everyday concepts related to the same phenomena. Scientific concepts develop "from the top down," that is, from verbal or mathematical formulae to their empirical correlates. Everyday concepts develop in the opposite direction "from the bottom up," from spontaneous impressions to more structured experiences: "In working its slow way upward, an everyday concept clears the path for a scientific concept in its downward development. It creates a series of structures necessary for the evolution of a concept's more primitive, elementary aspects, which gives it body and vitality. Scientific concepts, in turn, supply structures for the upward development of the child's spontaneous concepts toward consciousness and deliberate use" (Vygotsky, 1986, p. 194).

Vygotsky's followers in the Soviet Union further elaborated the distinction between scientific and everyday concepts into the notion of theoretical versus empirical learning (see Chapter 2). In the West the distinction between scientific and everyday concepts has attracted researchers' attention in connection with the widely discussed problem of the misconceptions held by students learning science and the more general problem of conceptual differences between novices and experts (Carey, 1985; Vosniadou, 1994).

The last of the problems discussed by Vygotsky (1986) in *Thought and Language* is the phenomenon of inner speech. He addressed this issue twice: the first time in the context of his critique of Piaget's notion of childhood egocentrism, and the second time in his discussion of the social meaning versus personal sense of the world. According to Piaget, the initial state of a child's thought can be characterized as autistic, that is, completely self-centered and oblivious to contradictions (Piaget, 1959, 1969). Later, under the influence of adults, the child starts changing his or her mental habits in the direction of greater rationality and decentration. Egocentric thought of the child represents a transitory stage, a certain compromise between original autism and logic. Egocentric speech is a speech-for-oneself that is mostly incomprehensible to others. It reflects the egocentric nature of the child's thought and the pleasure principle that guides it. In the course of the child's development egocentric speech dies out, giving way to socialized speech, which is related to the reality principle and is comprehensible to interlocutors.

Vygotsky, who replicated some of Piaget's experiments, insisted that the earliest speech of the child is already social. At a certain age this primitive social speech becomes divided into egocentric speech-for-oneself and communicative speech-for-others. Inner speech is a product of the transformation and internalization of this egocentric speech-for-oneself. Far from being a useless, disappearing phenomenon, egocentric speech is a necessary stage in the development of inner forms of verbal reasoning and self-regulation. Vygotsky's and Piaget's position are complementary in this respect. Piaget started with the premise that child's speech is individual and idiosyncratic, and attempted to show how it becomes socialized. Vygotsky started with the premise that inner psychological functions first appear as external relationships. For him the major problem was not in how the child acquires socialized speech, but rather in how communicative speech-for-others becomes the child's individualized speech-for-oneself. In this context the transition from egocentric to inner speech reveals the process of internalization of speech forms that had their roots in primitive communicative activity. Vygotsky explored the peculiar grammar and syntax of egocentric speech and linked them to the change in the addressee. While egocentric speech is still unconsciously oriented toward some external listener, inner speech is oriented toward the internal listener, that is, oneself, who does not need all the grammatical and syntactic forms that are indispensable in the overt dialogue.

As an illustration Vygotsky (1986, p. 237) presents a fragment from Leo Tolstoy's *Anna Karenina* (part IV, chap. 13). Communication between Kitty and Levin, who are in love and understand each other instantly, acquires the quality of inner speech, as if they were one person. Levin writes only the initial letters of words while declaring his love, but Kitty easily understands the sentence because she fully "participates" in Levin's train of thought.

The sociocultural approach to language development presupposed that different social settings must have a differential effect on the child's acquisition of speech. Unfortunately, Vygotsky was unable to develop this aspect of his research program. He only outlined it as a necessary complement to the "morphological" analysis of egocentric, communicative, and inner speech, mentioning that the coefficients of egocentric speech differ depending on the social contexts of the child's upbringing. Piaget's children in Geneva, children in German kindergartens, and Vygotsky's subjects in Moscow all had different social milieus and consequently different prevalent types of communication that shaped their verbal development.

Vygotsky's belief in the functional value of egocentric speech and the importance of sociocultural factors in its development has found additional support in more recent studies (Zivin, 1979; Diaz and Berk, 1992). Berk and Garvin (1984) demonstrate that the egocentric speech of children in poor Appalachian communities moves through the same sequence of changes as the egocentric speech of middle-class children, but more slowly. The authors suggest that this delay may reflect the more taciturn character of interpersonal interactions in Appalachian families, where parents rely more on gestures than words when communicating with their children. It was also shown that children who progressed more rapidly from self-guiding audible remarks to inner speech were more advanced in their task-related behavior.

Vygotsky returned to the issue of inner speech in the context of his discussion of sociocultural and individual aspects of word meaning. He made a distinction between the sociocultural meaning *(znachenie)* of a word, which reflects a generalized concept, and word sense *(smysl),* which depends on the context in which the word is used by an individual.

[Sense] is a dynamic, fluid, complex whole, which has several zones of unequal stability. Meaning is only one of the zones of sense, the most stable and precise zone. A word acquires its sense from the contexts in which it appears; in different contexts it changes its sense. The dictionary meaning of a word is no more than a stone in the edifice of sense, no more than a potentiality which finds diversified realization in speech. (Vygotsky, 1986, p. 245)

In inner speech the predominance of sense over meaning, sentence over word, and context over sentence is a rule. Whereas meaning stands for socialized speech, sense represents a borderline between one's individual and thus incommunicable thinking and verbal thought, which is dependent on culturally sanctioned word meanings. In inner speech two important processes become interwoven: the internalization and individuation of speech forms originating in external dialogues, and the translation of intimate thoughts into a form of speech comprehensible for others. Inner speech thus serves as an interface between culturally sanctioned symbolic systems and the idiosyncratic images and figures of individual thought. The interaction of sense and meaning constitutes the inner dialogue between two "coauthors" of one thought, that is, two sides of the self. One of these "coauthors" accommodates his or her thought to the preexistent system of meanings; the other "coauthor" immediately turns them into idiosyncratic senses that later will be again transformed into intelligible words. The "author" of thought therefore is simultaneously engaged in two conversations, one outbound, the other inbound. Outbound thought and speech are oriented toward real or imaginary interlocutors, while the inbound thought brings the meanings of others back to the subject. The coexistence of these inbound and outbound processes ensures the dialogical nature of human thought. In this sense inner speech provides a psychological image of the individual as a subject, as the initiator and source of thinking. The creative work of a writer becomes a model for psychological processes observed in inner speech.

In his study of inner speech Vygotsky reached the outer limits of the traditionally defined subject matter of psychology and began to redefine it. The work of a writer and the creation of literary texts appeared as a paradigm of sociocultural activity generative of human higher mental processes (Kozulin, 1993). This redefinition of psychology's subject put

Vygotsky outside the ranks of his contemporaries and created serious problems for the acceptance of his ideas in academic psychology. Some Vygotskian scholars even suggest that the novelty of Vygotsky's views was directly related to his status as an outsider to the field:

> The range of ideas introduced by Vygotsky, alien to traditional psychology, called for special means of discussion and analysis. And he drew many of these means from philology and linguistics. His position as a methodologist with regard to the whole of psychology, the historical view he held of it, close attention to the problem of the sign, a historical approach that was at the same time structural and the attempt to synthesize them—these are, in my view, the key points in the work and ideas of Vygotsky. It turned out that in the process [of this work] Vygotsky broke down the traditional object of psychology. His works were not psychological in a common meaning of the word; moreover, they practically destroyed the traditional object of psychological analysis. (Schedrovitsky, 1982, p. 62)

## Vygotsky's Followers: Elaborations and Revisions of the Principle of Activity

In the early 1930s two opposite trends affecting the dissemination of Vygotsky's ideas could be observed. On the one hand, Vygotsky became a recognized leader of a whole group of young psychologists who enthusiastically implemented his theory in a variety of experimental, educational, and clinical settings. On the other hand, the political climate associated with Stalin's ascension to power was becoming quite inhospitable to any independent-minded thinker, Vygotsky included, who dared to voice original ideas in the social sciences. Vygotsky's interest in psychoanalysis, Gestalt psychology, and the cross-cultural analysis of cognition was denounced as "anti-Marxist," "eclectic," and "erroneous." Vygotsky and Luria's field study of comparative cognition was attacked for its alleged bias against ethnic minorities (Kozulin, 1984).

Vygotsky, who was already seriously ill, continued working in Moscow until 1934, when tuberculosis led to his tragically early death. Even before this, a group of Vygotsky's students that included Leontiev, Zaporozhets, and Bozhovich decided to leave Moscow for the Ukrainian city of Kharkov, where they established a new research center. Studies conducted in Kharkov centered on the problem of the interiorization of external actions in the form of inner mental functions. The problem of the relationship between psychological activity and consciousness was resolved in the following way: "Development of the consciousness of a child occurs as a result of the development of the system of psychological operations, which in their turn, are determined by the actual relations between a child and reality" (Leontiev, 1983, p. 347).

This insistence on the "actual relations to reality" became a major source of revision of Vygotsky's theory undertaken by his followers in Kharkov. Cole observes, "As even a superficial reading of this work indicates, Leontiev and the young researchers who worked with him established a good deal of a distance between themselves and their teacher Vygotsky" (Cole, 1980, p. 5).

The Kharkovists' emphasis on practical activity as a source of psychological functions fit well into the Soviet ideological climate of the 1930s, which glorified concrete labor as a major source of the socialist transformation of the human being. Somewhat ironically, it was also closer to the Piagetian program of exploring the internalization of sensory-motor actions, rather than to the original Vygotskian emphasis on symbolic psychological tools. In their elaboration of the notion of practical activity the Kharkovites came up with the following statement:

> Thus, even in children of early preschool age, practical activity assumes a new property, intelligibility or rationality; and practical activity is transformed into practical and intellectual activity. In other words, practical-operational, or practical thinking emerges. This form of thinking is obviously not an independent, completely formed, theoretical activity at this stage of development. It exists within practical activity as an element of that activity and as one of the properties of that activity is inseparable from it. Consequently, practical intellectual activity contains in its rudimentary aspects certain theoretical elements, elements of thought. (Asnin, 1980, p. 27)

Asnin's statement is in agreement with Vygotsky's developmental thesis "from action to thought," and yet the experimental studies that stood behind Asnin's position focused more on the problem-solving generalization and transfer rather than on the effect of psychological tools. The role of symbolic mediators was played down by the Khark-ovites. The next step in their revisionism was a direct confrontation with Vygotsky's sociocultural theory:

> Indeed, one of the most basic of all problems, the conceptuali-zation of the nature of mind, was incorrectly resolved [by Vy-gotsky]. The central characteristic of the human mind was thought to be *mastery* of the natural or biological mind through the use of auxiliary psychological means. Vygotsky's fundamen-tal error is contained in this thesis, in which he misconstrued the Marxist conception of the historical and social determina-tion of the human mind. Vygotsky understood the Marxist perspective idealistically. The conditioning of the human mind by social and historical factors was reduced to the influence of human culture on the individual. The source of mental devel-opment was thought to be the interaction of the subject's mind with a cultural, ideal reality rather than his actual relationship to reality. (Zinchenko, 1984, pp. 66–67)

Zinchenko thus claimed that practical activity provides a media-tion between the individual and reality, whereas Vygotsky emphasized that such an activity, in order to fulfill its role of mediator, must neces-sarily include symbolic psychological tools. Further, Zinchenko criti-cized the Vygotskian dichotomy of natural versus cultural psychological functions. In his opinion such a dichotomy ruined any attempt at un-derstanding the psychological aspect of the early stages of the child's development as distinct from the physiological. Finally Zinchenko at-tacks the notion of symbolic tools/mediators:

> He [Vygotsky] began with the thesis that the mastery of the sign-means was the basic and unique feature of human memory processes. He considered the central feature of any activity of remembering to be the relationship of the means to the object of this activity. But in Vygotsky's thinking, the relationship of the means to the object was divorced from the subject's relation-ship to reality considered in its actual and complete content. In the strict sense, the relationship between the means and the object was a logical rather than psychological relationship. But the history of social development cannot be reduced to the history of the development of culture. Similarly, we cannot reduce the development of human mind—the development of memory in particular—to the development of the relationships

of "external" and "internal" means to the object of activity. The history of cultural development must be included in the history of society's social and economic development; it must be considered in the context of the particular social and economic relationships that determine the origin and development of culture. In precisely this sense, the development of "theoretical" or "ideal" mediation must be considered in the context of the subject's real, practical relationships with reality, in the context of that which actually determines the origin, the development, and the content of mental activity. (Zinchenko, 1984, p. 70)

Thus the dividing line between Vygotsky and his followers in Kharkov fell between the cultural and the social aspects of sociocultural psychology. For Kharkovites the social portion associated with practical activity in a given social context seemed more important than those cultural means of mediation that according to Vygotsky are responsible for the transformation of natural psychological functions into a cultural one. In reality, however, the research program of the Kharkovites was rather detached from the social factors that they proclaimed as decisive. Their experimental design was quite traditional. For example, in Zinchenko's (1984) study of the influence of the child's goal-directed activity on his or her memorization, the accidental learning of the child was shown to lead to remembering either numbers or pictures depending on the overall task (either to arrange cards according to their numbers, or to classify them according to their content images). An important issue of specific goal-directed activities as generative of the child's psychological processes was explored in these studies. The cultural aspect of Vygotsky's theory, however, was neglected. Moreover, concrete activity (classification, problem solving, sensory-motor coordination, and so on) studies by Kharkovites remained detached from the social and economic relationships that were supposed to play the decisive role in human development. The task of filling this gap and elaborating the overall structure of the revised activity theory was taken up by Leontiev.

## Leontiev's Theory of Activity

Leontiev (1978, 1981) suggested a model for the analysis of human activity. Activities correspond to their motives, actions correspond to more specific goals, and operations are dependent on conditions: "Various concrete activities can be classified according to whatever features are convenient . . . However, the main feature that distinguishes one activity from another is its object. After all, it is precisely an activity's object that gives it a specific direction. In accordance with the terminology I have proposed, an activity's object is its real motive" (Leontiev, 1981, p. 59).

Leontiev observed that in human society the relationship between the individual and the object is not immediate but is mediated by collective experience and division of labor. For example, while food might be a primary object and motive of activity, this does not imply that the action of a particular individual is directed immediately at obtaining food. In the context of food-motivated activity the individual's contribution is partial, as dictated by the division of labor. Some individuals, for example, may concern themselves exclusively with the production of agricultural or hunting tools and participate in a food activity only in this indirect way:

> The isolation of goals and the formation of actions subordinated to them lead to a division of functions that were formerly interwoven in the motive. Of course, the motive fully retains its energizing function, but the directive function is another matter. The actions that constitute activity are energized by its motive, but are directed toward a goal . . . The selection of goal-directed actions as the components of concrete activities naturally raises the question of how these components are internally connected. As we have already mentioned, activity is not an additive process. Likewise, actions are not the special "parts" that constitute activity. Human activity exists only in the form of action or a chain of actions. For example, labor activity consists of labor actions, educational activity consists of educational actions, social interaction consists of acts of social interaction, etc. If we mentally tried to abstract actions from the activity that they translate into reality, nothing would remain. This may also be expressed as follows: when a concrete process—external or internal—unfolds before us, from the point of view of its motive, it is human activity, but in terms of subordination to a goal, it is an action or a chain of actions. (Leontiev, 1981, pp. 60–61)

In creating such a theoretical framework Leontiev was confronted with three formidable tasks: (1) elaborating the relations between labor activity and its reflection in psychological functions; (2) identifying the relations between labor-related motives and interpersonal motives in a given sociocultural context; and (3) identifying the composition of leading activities across the life span and their relation to emergent (or regressing) psychological processes.

Working within the sociocultural and political constraints of his time, Leontiev was hardly capable of thoroughly exploring the true motives underlying human activities. Whatever his original intentions, he produced no research that would elucidate the sociocultural influence of labor on cognition. In developing his theoretical schema Leontiev employed two conceptual languages: one was used on the activity level and the other on action and operations level. In discussing human activities Leontiev employed the categories of Marxist social philosophy such as production, appropriation, objectification, and disobjectification. The subject presumed by the use of these categories was the socio-historical, and therefore psychologically rather abstract, subject. Actions and operations were studied within the psychological paradigm, which had no immediate linkage to the higher-order social categories. One may suggest that what was missing from Leontiev's model was precisely the stratum of culture, emphasized by Vygotsky and neglected by his followers, which could provide a link between individual action and the social system that gives it its meaning.

By rejecting semiotic mediation and by insisting on the dominant role of practical actions Leontiev forced himself to elaborate the connection between the Marxist categories of production and objectification, and the psychological category of action. Even the most sophisticated of Western Marxists succeeded in doing this only in the form of a critique of the alienation of human action in capitalist society. The Marxists were remarkably unsuccessful in depicting the positive, creative aspects of human action as conditioned by a social system. This lack of success used to be explained as a reflection of the true condition prevalent in capitalist society, the condition of alienation. Unalienated, free action was reserved for future socialist life. Leontiev could not use this argument because he was studying people in what was called a "state of accomplished socialism." He chose to avoid the psychological discussion of these issues altogether, delivering instead the standard ideological verbiage about the alienation of the human mind in the capitalist world versus its free development in socialist Russia (Leontiev, 1981). In the context of later developments prompted by glasnost and perestroika in Russia this aspect of Leontiev's theory is deficient.

## Vygotsky Rediscovered

From the mid-1930s through the mid-1950s Vygotsky's works were blacklisted in the Soviet Union, and even his closest associates were unable to acknowledge the influence of their mentor. This posthumous ban was prompted in part by the Stalinist rejection of all works that conducted an open-minded dialogue with Western authors (as Vygotsky did); on a more specific level the ban was triggered by Stalin's attack against the psychoeducational assessment and testing movement known as "paedology." Many of Vygotsky's papers were published in paedological journals and thus became guilty by association (Kozulin, 1984; Van der Veer and Valsiner, 1991).

In the late 1950s this situation changed. Vygotsky's works were politically "rehabilitated" in the course of de-Stalinization, and it became fashionable to be considered his disciple.

Vygotsky's former students became solidly established at Moscow University and the Psychological Institute. Leontiev became the dean of the university's school of psychology. Under these circumstances it was not difficult for him to gain the status of official interpreter of Vygotsky's ideas, and his texts enjoyed a wider circulation than Vygotsky's original works. Gradually Vygotsky came to be regarded as a mere predecessor of Leontiev's theory of activity, and his emphasis on psychological tools was viewed as a deviation eventually rectified in Leontiev's writings.

In the late 1970s, however, Leontiev's theory began to be scrutinized more critically. An important role in this reevaluation was played by the discovery of some of Vygotsky's papers in the course of the preparation of the six volumes of his *Collected Works* (Vygotsky, 1982–1984). Leontiev's theory, which had become an all-embracing psychological doctrine, ran into the same trouble that Vygotsky had warned against in his early paper dedicated to the issue of consciousness (Vygotsky, 1979). The notion of activity in Leontiev's theory was used both as an explanatory principle and as a subject of concrete psychological study. As a result the phenomena of human activity became "explained" by referring to the principle of activity. This returned Vygotsky's followers to the same vicious circle of tautology about which their teacher spoke when he criticized mentalism for its "explanation" of the phenomena of consciousness through the principle of consciousness, and behaviorism for its attempts to "explain" the phenomena of behavior through the principle of behavior.

Critical evaluation of Leontiev's theory led to further elaboration of the notion of activity. It was emphasized that activity as an explanatory principle presupposes that individual behavior and consciousness appear as "organs" of superindividual, sociocultural activity. Individual psychological activity could also become a subject of scientific investigation. But in this case—and this is a crucial point—the structural elements elaborated for activity in its capacity as an explanatory principle will be irrelevant. One concept of activity cannot successfully carry out both functions simultaneously. But this is precisely what happened in Leontiev's theory. The structural elements of activity, activity-motive, action-goal, and operation-conditions—once proposed in the context of an explanatory principle—were used in the context of the subject of study. In Vygotsky's original theory higher mental functions served as subjects of study, psychological tools as mediators, and activity as the explanatory principle. In the work of his followers, activity and actions began to play all these roles simultaneously. The "rediscovery" of Vygotsky in the Soviet Union became associated with greater attention to the cultural aspects of his theory, his metatheoretical analysis of the crises in psychology, and educational applications of his notion of scientific concepts (Kozulin, 1990a; Wertsch, 1991).

Vygotsky's "rediscovery" in the Soviet Union coincided with his much delayed "discovery" by Western psychologists. The acceptance of Vygotsky's theory in the West was neither simple nor unconditional. Several factors contributed to this delayed process of recognition. Vygotsky's texts possess a certain literary quality that created serious problems for translators. His terminology did not coincide with that traditionally used in the English-language psychological literature. The fact that Vygotsky was a theoretician par excellence also did not gain him many points among the more pragmatic and empirically oriented of his Western readers. In the end, however, the well-known maxim that "there is nothing more practical than a good theory" proved to be correct in his case.

The cross-cultural study of cognition benefited greatly from Vygotsky's sociocultural approach. Instead of simply focusing on similarities and differences in the cognitive processes of individuals belonging to different cultures, psychologists like Michael Cole (Cole et al., 1971; Cole and Scribner, 1974) put these differences into appropriate sociocultural contexts. First the role of literacy, as a system of symbolic tools, was scrutinized with respect to its possible cognitive outcomes. Then literacy as such had to be differentiated from the overall system of formal schooling, which presupposes special types of a child's activity that go beyond a simple ability to decode or encode written texts. Cole (1990) concluded that the cognitive consequences of formal education and the use of psychological tools associated with it are not absolute but depend strongly on the structure of activities predominant in a given culture or subculture. The role of school-based cognitive skills becomes more important with the increase in demand for "scholastic" types of activities outside school.

Another significant influence of Vygotsky can be observed in studies focusing on learning situations and the agency of learning (Wertsch, Tulviste, and Hagstrom 1993). While traditional approaches almost instinctively identify the agency of learning as belonging to an individual, the sociocultural approach offers an alternative view. In Vygotskian theories agency is understood as extending beyond the individual. This extension occurs in two major forms: (a) agency is often a property of dyads and other small groups rather than individuals, and (b) symbolic cultural tools that mediate human action are inherently connected to historical, cultural, and institutional settings, thus extending human agency beyond the given individual. These theoretical positions were translated into a number of practical applications. Various forms of shared, collaborative, and reciprocal learning situations were identified. It was shown that both psychoeducational assessment and instruction provide more valuable information and lead to better results when students are engaged in assisted learning activities (Brown and Ferrara, 1985). These activities help the child to actualize those cognitive processes that belong to what Vygotsky called a zone of proximal development (ZPD). These processes are not yet manifest, but can be actualized under conditions of shared or reciprocal learning activity. In the works of Rogoff (1990) the metaphor of apprenticeship became a guiding principle in exploring and identifying various interactive activities carried out by children, their more competent peers, and adults that ultimately lead to the appropriation by children of those modes of action that are valuable in a given sociocultural milieu.

Finally, Vygotskian approaches inserted a new perspective into the protracted argument between empiricists versus constructivists regarding the nature of school-based concept formation in children (Hatano, 1993). Here again the issue of activity came to the forefront. From a Vygotskian point of view the child neither internalizes concepts in a ready-made form nor constructs them independently on the basis of his or her own experience. For proper concept formation the child should become involved in specially designed learning activities that provide a framework for guided construction.

In the 1990s Vygotskian theory became more widely accepted in Western psychology and education than ever before. This acceptance coincided with a certain shift of emphasis in Western psychology itself from behavioral process studies in the laboratory to such sociocultural phenomena as informal and classroom learning, first- and second-language acquisition, job-related problem solving, practical intelligence, and so on. Vygotsky's emphasis on the role played by symbolic mediators in the development of human cognition found its way into new theories of literacy and learning (Olson, 1994; Egan, 1997). Classroom applications of Vygotskian ideas began to appear with increasing frequency (Moll, 1990; Dixon-Krauss, 1996). Thus the notion of psychological activity, which for a long time had been perceived as an internal matter of Soviet and Russian psychology, became a challenge for the international community of psychologists as a whole.

# 2 ～

# Piaget, Vygotsky, and the Cognitive Revolution

The cognitive revolution in learning theory and educational psychology, as acknowledged by the majority of American psychologists (Horowitz, 1989), has occurred as the culmination of a lengthy and arduous process. For quite some time behaviorist and psychoanalytic theories were in the limelight while cognitive approaches remained in the shadows. By the same token, children's thinking was almost universally perceived as a reflection of their individual abilities, while social and cultural characteristics of the learning process were either taken for granted or ignored. In both cases they remained beyond the scope of learning theory.

The reversal of fortune in this cognitive and sociocultural revolution is associated with the contributions of two great psychologists, Jean Piaget of Switzerland and Lev Vygotsky of Russia. Both made their first significant contributions to psychology in the 1920s, but in English-speaking countries true renown did not come until the 1960s for Piaget and even later, in the 1980s, for Vygotsky. This late recognition underscores the universal value of the contributions made by these psychologists: their theories address the fundamental problems of child development and learning and do not aim at providing quick answers that follow current fashion in popular science or education.

In this chapter I review the commonalities and the differences between the basic premises of Piagetian and Vygotskian theories. Their common denominators include a child-centered approach, an emphasis on action in the formation of thought, and a systemic understanding of psychological functioning. Differences are reflected in the Piagetians' focus on the inner restructuring of children's thought and the Vygot-skians' emphasis on the formative influence of the sociocultural model upon this thought. Illustrations showing the application of these ideas in the classroom will make these differences more tangible.

## Common Ground in Vygotsky's and Piaget's Theories

For a variety of reasons, Piaget and Vygotsky are most often presented as scientific antagonists, and their views as negating each other. Although it is true that many differences exist in their understanding of psychological development and learning, it is more advantageous to acknowledge that there are similarities in their positions and that these elements have become the cornerstones of the cognitive revolution we are now experiencing.

### Child-Centered Psychology

Acknowledging Piaget's revolutionary impact on child psychology, Vygotsky (1986) wrote: "Like many another great discovery, Piaget's idea is simple to the point of seeming self-evident. It had already been expressed in the words of J. J. Rousseau, which Piaget himself quoted, that a child is not a miniature adult and his mind is not the mind of an adult on a small scale" (p. 13).

The idea appears simple unless one realizes its theoretical consequences. Above all, the popular behaviorist search for the universal building blocks of behavior similar in children, adults, and animals becomes senseless in this perspective. J. B. Watson's (1970) thesis that "all complex behavior is a growth or development out of simple responses" (p. 137) loses its attractive simplicity. If a child's behavior is qualitatively different, then linear extrapolation from "simple responses" is misleading, and it is erroneous to search for small-scale copies of adult behavior in children. The traditional notion of universal thought processes that are underdeveloped in a child fares no better. As Edouard Claparede observed in his preface to Piaget's first book: "After all, the error has been, if I am not mistaken, that in examining child thought we have applied to it the mould and pattern of the adult thought" (Claparede, 1959, pp. x–xi).

In retrospect, Piaget's insight into the unique and self-important character of children's thought fits reasonably well into the more general pattern of structuralist ideas that were taking hold of the social and behavioral sciences from the 1930s to the 1960s (Kozulin, 1978). In zoopsychology, ethologists promoted the idea of species-specific behavior that cannot be reduced to such universal elements as conditional reflexes or stimulus-response pairs. In anthropology, early attempts to portray so-called primitive cultures as qualitatively similar but developmentally inferior to European culture were challenged by a relativistic approach that focused on the self-important and unique characteristics of each culture. In psychology itself Heinz Werner (1965) promoted the idea of the irreducible character of different cognitive structures in such subjects of psychological investigation as children, mental patients, and "primitive" people.

## From Action to Thought

The second issue on which Piaget and Vygotsky were in agreement concerns the relationship between action and thought. Classical mentalistic psychology presumed the primacy of thought over action in such a way that action was perceived only as a realized thought. An individual was first supposed to have an idea of a certain solution and only then to realize it in a chosen act. Thought, in its turn, was considered primarily as a representation of reality, rather than as the means of acting upon it. In his theory of sensory-motor intelligence, Piaget (1969) challenged this position. He demonstrated that thought itself has an operational structure derived from actual behavior performed by the child. For example, by physically putting objects together or by separating them, a child, in a form of action, performs what later will be internalized as the mental operations of addition and subtraction. Thus the key to the child's thinking lies not in *sui generis* ideas but in the child's practical activity, which in the course of development becomes internalized and transformed into cognitive operations.

While in agreement with Piaget concerning the formula "from action to thought," Vygotsky made an important amendment to it. In

Piagetian theory action appears first and foremost as a spontaneous physical interaction between the child and physical objects. Later in life the child becomes capable of substituting words and logical formulae for these physical interactions, and in this way arrives at symbolic operational thought. Vygotsky argued that such a picture does not correspond to the reality in which child development takes place. The child's interaction with objects is always only one element in a wider activity that is socially and historically specific (Vygotsky, 1978; Kozulin, 1986, 1990a). This activity is organized and controlled by society and its representatives. Parents infuse even the earliest of the child's operations with meaning that has not only individual but sociocultural connotations. The formula "from action to thought" should therefore take into account the sociocultural nature of action and its development and internalization in children.

## Systemic Organization of the Child's Thought

Both Piaget and Vygotsky argued against the popular attempt to present the child's mind as a sack filled with discrete cognitive skills and pieces of information. Both sought a systemic explanation of cognitive functioning. In Piagetian theory systemic explanation is based on two major notions, the notion of a group of operations and the notion of the developmental stage. Individual operations always appear as elements of the whole, and their nature is determined by the nature of this whole system. An isolated operation is an abstraction. "A single operation could not be an operation, because the peculiarity of operations is that they form systems. Here we may well protest vigorously against logical atomism, whose pattern has been a grievous hindrance to the psychology of thought" (Piaget, 1969, p. 35). Classical mentalistic psychology, like classical logic, speaks of concepts as elements of thought. It is clear, however, that any concept depends on other concepts, that is, on a system. This dependence, moreover, is expressed in terms of operation. A concept such as "class" cannot exist by itself. It necessarily requires the notion of "classification," and the former grows out of the latter, because only operations of classification can engender particular classes. In isolation from such a system, "class" will remain an intuitive collection rather than a "class" in the true meaning of this concept. The same is true for other concepts, such as that of asymmetrical relations; for example, $A < B$ is impossible in isolation from the system of serial relationships $A < B < C < D$ and so forth. "In short, in any possible domain of constituted thought psychological reality consists of complex operational systems and not isolated operations conceived as elements prior to these systems" (Piaget, 1969, p. 36).

This same idea of a system as a whole guided Piaget in his concept of the developmental stage. Piaget distinguished four major stages: sensory-motor, intuitive, concrete operational, and formal operational. At each of these stages, which, according to Piaget, appear in a strict developmental order, the child is acting in a way characteristic of a respective level of cognitive development. For example, different schemas of pre-operational thought belong to one system that at this level endows a child's reasoning with a certain consistency and homogeneity.

Vygotsky approached this same problem of the systemic organization of children's thought from the point of view of the relationships among different psychological functions. He pointed out that, while psychological functions such as perception, memory, or logical reasoning in themselves may change very little during childhood, their relationships do. For example, in younger children reasoning often plays a subordinate role to memory—a child reasons by remembering concrete instances or episodes. In adolescents this relationship is often reversed—the task of remembering some item is transformed by an adolescent into a reasoning task. The adolescent logically constructs the sequence of events that ultimately leads him or her to the item to be recalled. Only at this late stage is memory in its pure form called into service.

The same is true for the verbal function. According to Vygotsky, the development of both thinking and speech in childhood depends primarily on the changing relationships between these two functions that enter into the different types of systemic relationships with each other. "It was shown and proved experimentally that mental development does not coincide with the development of separate psychological functions, but rather depends on changing relations between them. The development of each function, in turn, depends upon the progress in the development of the interfunctional system" (Vygotsky, 1986, p. 167). Psychological development, therefore, is envisaged by Vygotsky as a construction of ever more complex systems of different psychological functions that work in cooperation to mediate one another. The failure to form an interfunctional system manifests itself as a learning disability or even more severe forms of cognitive retardation (Luria, 1960).

## Differences between Piaget and Vygotsky: Cognitive Individualism versus the Sociocultural Approach

Now that the common ground for what constitutes the cognitive revolution has been established, it is possible to distinguish between Piagetian and Vygotskian theoretical positions and to inquire into the consequences of these differences for educational practice. Probably the most essential difference lies in their understanding of the subject of psychological activity. For Piaget, this subject is an individual child whose mind, through interaction with the physical and social world, arrives at the mature forms of reasoning associated with formal operations. For Vygotsky, psychological activity has sociocultural characteristics from the very beginning of development; children, therefore, are not lone discoverers of logical rules, but individuals who master their own psychological processes through tools offered by a given culture. The following stories, one reported by Piaget and the other by Vygotsky, underscore the difference in their understanding of what constitutes a paradigmatic learning situation.

> You may recall Piaget's account of a mathematician friend who inspired his studies in the conservation of number. This man told Piaget about an incident from childhood, where he counted a number of pebbles he had set out in a line. Having counted them from left to right and found there were 10, he decided to see how many there would be if he counted them from right to left. Intrigued to find that there were still 10, he put them in a different arrangement and counted them again. He kept rearranging and counting them until he decided that, no matter what the arrangement, he was always going to find that there were ten. Number is independent of the order of counting . . . I think that it must be that the whole enterprise was his [child's] own wonderful idea. He raised the question for himself and figured out for himself how to try to answer it. (Duckworth, 1987, pp. 4–5)

Vygotsky (1978, pp. 33–35), in contrast, reports the following observations. He asked four- and five-year-old children to press one of five keys on a keyboard in response to picture stimuli. Because the task exceeded the children's natural capabilities, it caused serious difficulties for them. Moreover, the whole process of selection was carried out in a motor sphere—the child made a selection from possible movements instead of first arriving at a certain decision and then realizing it in a movement. This type of activity changed dramatically when an auxiliary system of signs attached to keys was introduced. Although on the surface the task became more complex because in addition to stimuli and keys the children were supposed to pay attention to signs, the result was impressive. Children ceased to respond with a sequence of hesitant or impulsive movements, developing instead an internal decision-making procedure linked to a sign, with movement used to implement an already-made decision. The natural form of activity was replaced by the activity mediated by artificial signs that were introduced by adults and that reflected their system of cultural tools.

These two vignettes are sufficient to pinpoint the major difference in Vygotsky's and Piaget's attitudes toward learning. For Piaget, learning occurs in an unassisted interaction between the child's mental schemas and the objects of the external world. As a result, the child is having "wonderful ideas" of his or her own. The only requirement for the learning milieu is that it be sufficiently rich so that children have enough objects and processes to practice their schemas. Alternatively, from Vygotsky's point of view, learning occurs in the collaboration between children and the adults who introduce symbolic tools-mediators to children and teach them how to organize and control their natural psychological functions through these cultural tools. In the process, the natural psychological functions of the child change, their nature becoming culturally and socially informed and organized.

The same difference in attitudes is reflected in the choice of an assessment situation. For Piaget an ideal testing of the child's reasoning occurs when the child is confronted with an unfamiliar problem or task. Only where specific knowledge is absent may one hope to identify the "infantile" way of reasoning unaffected by the imitation of adult logic. Vygotsky, on the contrary, considered a collaborative situation to be paradigmatic. For that reason he strongly criticized standard psychometric methods that take into account only the manifest level of the child's performance. This manifest level is then interpreted as reflecting the intellectual development of the child. Vygotsky argued that two children whose manifest level corresponds, for example, to the mental age of eight, may have very different learning potentials, and that these learning potentials rather than actual performance levels are indicative of the future success or failure of these children in school learning. To measure these learning potentials, children are given somewhat more difficult but similar tasks and are provided with assistance in the form of orientation in the task, a leading question, and so on. If one of the children can perform with assistance at the level of the mental age of twelve, and the other one at the level of nine, we may conclude that the zone of proximal development (ZPD) for the first child is four, while for the second is just one year. Vygotsky concluded that it would be erroneous to claim that the level of intellectual development is similar in the two children. "Experience has shown that the child with the larger zone of proximal development will do much better in school. This measure gives a more helpful clue than mental age does to the dynamics of intellectual processes" (Vygotsky, 1986, p. 187).

In recent years the notion of dynamic assessment based on the principle of the ZPD has captured the attention of many American psychologists (Lidz, 1987b). Apart from assessment techniques, ZPD helped to establish the notion of collaborative learning. In collaborative learning the child is neither a passive recipient of knowledge offered by the teacher nor an independent thinker who arrives at his or her own solutions, but rather a participant in learning activities shared by children and adults (Rogoff and Wertsch, 1984; Newman, Griffin, and Cole, 1989). Independently of the Vygotskian tradition, a somewhat similar approach to learning potential and its dynamic assessment has been developed in Israel by Reuven Feuerstein (Feuerstein, Rand, and Hoffman, 1979). A comparison of ZPD-based assessment and Feuerstein's methods will be provided in Chapter 3.

## The Role of Language

Piaget's early recognition as a new force in child psychology owes much to his first books dedicated to the problem of child speech. There is a certain irony in such a beginning, since in his mature works Piaget avoided the issue of language. Some of his followers in the field of education even made one's attitude toward language into a litmus test, separating Piagetians who emphasize thinking from "traditionalists" who focus on verbal development. "The general conclusion which I press on you," wrote Hans Furth in *Piaget for Teachers* (1970, p. 65), "is not to exaggerate the role of language in the development of thinking." Wadsworth (1978, p. 126) also believed that reading is not essential for cognitive development:

> Reading is an important skill, but it is not a necessary skill for cognitive development to proceed. Children can attain the development of formal operations without learning to read. Development during the preoperational and concrete operational periods depends on the child's actions on objects and events in his environment. These actions are the materials from which mental structures evolve. Reading, writing, or arithmetic skills do not contribute to this process. The child's actions are still central. When formal operations are developed, the child becomes capable of using reading skills in constructing mental operations.

For Vygotsky, language in its different forms constitutes the central theme of cognitive development. For him, cognitive development can be imagined as a dynamic pattern of engagements and separations between intellectual and verbal functions. Rather than a merger of two "strings," the relationship between language and thought looks more like a knotted line with threads from one string being interwoven into the other after each knot.

The dynamic character of the relationships between thought and language may sometimes give an impression of a certain "regression" on the part of the child's language. For example, children's first steps in written language are made when their oral speech is already quite well developed. As a result their writing appears as a "regression" in its pure verbal quality. At the same time, writing involves cognitive elements that are still missing in oral exchanges. While much in oral exchanges is carried out unconsciously, writing necessitates closer attention to the formal properties of language, requires more careful planning, and puts additional emphasis on the self-conscious motivation of the writer's activity.

The same apparent "regression" associated with the transition to a new stage of verbal activity is manifest in the phenomenon of so-called egocentric speech in younger children. Egocentric or private speech is not addressed or adapted to a listener and is carried on by the child with apparent satisfaction in the absence of any response from others. From Piaget's (1959) perspective egocentric speech is but a mere verbal accompaniment of the child's egocentric thought that is insensitive to contradictions and does not take into account the point of view of others. The fate of the child's egocentric speech is to disappear, being replaced by socialized speech attuned to the expectations of the listener. Vygotsky (1986) challenged this position, arguing that although private speech looks immature when compared with the communicative speech of the same child, it nevertheless is cognitively superior to it. Through a series of simple but ingenious experiments Vygotsky was able to show that instead of being a mere accompaniment of immature thought private speech serves as a precursor of the silent inner speech that serves as an important tool of a child's reasoning. When confronted with a difficult task the child significantly increases the amount of his or her private speech utterances that help in problem solving. These early findings of Vygotsky have been confirmed in more recent studies (Zivin, 1979).

The current research literature (Cromer, 1991) continues to register an ongoing debate between those who believe that cognitive structures come first and support the progress of language, and those who insist that language has its own more or less independent course of development. The truth may lie between these two extremes: "Our cognitive abilities at different stages of development make certain meanings *available* for expression. But, in addition, we must also possess certain specifically linguistic capabilities in order to come to express these meanings in language . . . Though language development depends on cognition, language has its own specific sources . . . It appears that much of what is being discovered during the current vogue of psycholinguistic research supports Vygotsky's view" (Cromer, 1991, p. 54).

## The Piagetian System in the Classroom

One of the important consequences of the Piagetian revolution in learning theory is the change in teachers' attitude toward children's thinking.

The following is a paraphrase of Eleanor Duckworth's (1987, pp. 89–92) account of her work with primary school children. The problem offered to the children was a classical one from Piaget, Inhelder, and Szeminska (1981) known as "The Island." Each child received a solid clay block, 4" high and 3" × 3" square (see Figure 2.1a); a pile of small (1") wooden cubes; and a blue board meant to be a lake on which there are three patches of cardboard meant to be islands—one 4" × 3", one 3" × 2", and one 2" × 2". Children were told that the solid block was an apartment building that had to be vacated by its occupants. With the help of the small cubes children were asked to build a new building to accommodate

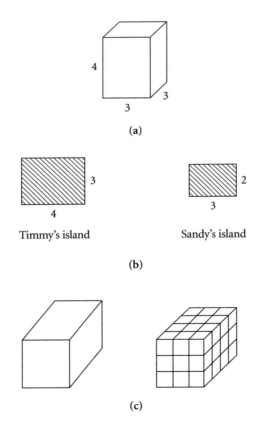

Figure 2.1 Adapted from E. Duckworth, *"The Having of Wonderful Ideas" and Other Essays on Teaching and Learning* (New York: Teachers College Press, © 1987 by Teachers College, Columbia University, all rights reserved), pp. 88, 91.

the occupants on one of the islands. The base of the new building was to cover the entire island; it could not go off into the water, and the new building had to have as much room as the original one. One of the children, Timmy, received a task with the 4" × 3" island; the other child, Sandy, received the 3" × 2" island (Figure 2.1b).

First the children tried to build new buildings of the same height as the model. As a result Sandy had to acknowledge that his building has less room than the model, and Timmy that his had a bit more room than the model. At that moment Duckworth intervened by taking a model and turning it on its side in such a way that its base became the same as Timmy's (Figure 2.1c). The children immediately acknowledged that now the buildings were equal. When, however, Duckworth turned the model upright again, Timmy said that more blocks should be added to his new building. After comparing the model and his building a number of times, Timmy arrived at the conclusion that while the model was "bigger," his building was "wider." After that Timmy started measuring with his hands both the model and the new building. As a result of this operation he came to the conclusion that the model was taller by the same amount as his building was wider. Then attention was turned to Sandy's building. After a number of attempts the children settled on a building that had five layers on a 3" × 2" base (that is, one layer short of the correct solution).

In her analysis, Duckworth suggested that the children began with the idea of judging the overall amount of space by its most salient dimension, the height. Then they were able to appreciate the fact that a greater size in one dimension (height) could be compensated by a smaller size in another (width). The idea of compensation, however, was applied only to a single dimension, rather than a two-dimensional slice. Children apparently perceived the model as a solid entity, and were unable to imagine it as a composite of units that could be calculated.

The above analysis has a direct relation to Piagetian ideas about the epistemology of volume. Of the kind of work that Timmy and Sandy did, he said:

> In all these trends, there is growth in the articulation of Euclid-
> ean intuitions of volume. It is through that increasing articula-
> tion that notions of volume lose their topological character and
> come to conform with Euclidean notions of length and area

which are elaborated at this level. However, although these articulations pave the way for operational handling of the various relations together with their logical multiplication, they are insufficient to enable children to effect those reversible compositions which mark the operational level proper. Thus these responses are intermediate in character, and this fact appears most clearly in the answers given to our questions about conservation. (Piaget, Inhelder, and Szeminska, 1981, p. 369)

Duckworth emphasized that this kind of work with children is useful and important beyond its conformity to the Piagetian theoretical model. The main thing is the focus on how children are making sense of the problem in their own way: "Piaget's contribution here, are, on the one hand, having located what is essentially crucial intellectual issues for children, and finding ways to put the issues in the form that catches their interest; and on the other hand, developing the 'clinical interview' technique in which the adult role is to find out as much as possible about what the child believes about the issue. Both these aspects are what gave the session with Timmy and Sandy its significance" (Duckworth, 1987, p. 92).

## The Vygotskian System in the Classroom

According to Vygotskian theory, one of the most important changes that should be produced in the child when he or she enters the formal schooling framework is the change in the child's *position* (Elkonin, 1971). From a "natural" position as a son or daughter, or playmate, the child exits to the rather artificial position of a student. The artificiality of this position is deliberate. In everyday life the child uses his or her cognition directly and naturally in order to achieve certain results (practical activity) or to enjoy the activity itself (play). In the formal learning situation this direct application of cognitive resources becomes suspended. Children do not solve problems at school because results of this problem solving are important, and they do not learn to write because the lines of words they produce are needed. Children do this in order to master their own cognitive apparatus, in order to be able to plan, control, and evaluate their own actions. Formal schooling, therefore, aims at the deliberate "denaturalization" of the students' position, so that children can make their own actions a subject of their own deliberate analysis and control.

For the child it is not always easy to assume this new position of student and accept learning activity as a dominant one. According to Vygotskians, there is no reason to take this lack of positional flexibility as inevitable. On the contrary, special activities should be designed for the period of the child's development as he or she concludes kindergarten and starts school. These activities are aimed at developing a *dynamic position* in the child, that is, the ability to approach objects and processes from different positions. This position is a necessary prerequisite for the child's successful involvement in the learning activity. Here I will describe one of the methods widely used by Elkonin's research group (Bugrimenko and Elkonin, 1994).

The method is based on providing a child with "magic glasses," which according to the rules of the game allow the child to see only some of the object's parameters. For example, the child is shown a sequence of squares that differ both in size and in color (for example, black, dark grey, light grey). The task is to find squares matching the model ones in a pool of different geometric figures of a different color. The role of magic glasses ("you cannot see colors, only shapes and sizes") is to suspend the child's immediate response, which often leads to the selection of the matching figure by one parameter (size) only. The child learns to assume an artificial position that then is turned into the opposite ("you can see only colors"). As a result children who received this kind of training not only demonstrated a superior level in solving Piagetian logical multiplication (size × color) problems, but also displayed the mastery of positional flexibility by indicating for themselves "Now, as in the glasses" and only then proceeding toward solution.

Acquisition of a number of skills that pose particular difficulties for primary school students can be facilitated if the paradigm of psychological tools is used. The symbolic character of psychological tools allows for generalized skill acquisition. Instead of learning a particular task or operation the child acquires a more general principle applicable to different tasks. Such a generalized approach becomes possible through the development of symbolic representational models of the whole group of tasks. Consider the following example of psychological tools developed by Diachenko and summarized by Karpov (1995).

The target of primary school classroom activity is story comprehension. To facilitate students' acquisition of this important skill, the students first learn the mechanism of arbitrary symbolic representation of various story characters. For example, when a story about three bears is read by the teacher, students are asked to display sticks of a different length each time one of the three bears is mentioned. During the next stage students learn to place colored tokens representing different story characters on their desks following the appearance of these characters in the story read by the teacher. After that the students perform an opposite task. Being shown certain combinations of tokens, they recall an appropriate episode of the story. The next step is to present the child with a sequence of plastic frames representing different episodes of an unknown story, place specifically designated character tokens within these frames, and ask the child to generate a story using the supplied structure. Finally, the students are taught to create a story structure by drawing episode frames and filling them with signs-characters. As a result of these activities students demonstrated much better comprehension of the story structure not only while using psychological tools but also in the absence of these tools, which indicates that the psychological tool action had become internalized by the students in the form of inner mental schema.

One of the most educationally potent notions developed by Vygotskians is the distinction between "spontaneous" and "scientific" concepts (Vygotsky, 1986). Spontaneous concepts emerge from the child's own reflections on immediate, everyday experiences; they are rich but unsystematic and highly contextual. Scientific concepts originate in the structured and specialized activity of classroom instruction and are characterized by systemic and logical organization. The concepts themselves do not necessarily relate to scientific issues—they may represent historical, linguistic, or practical knowledge—but their organization is "scientific" in the sense of having a formal, logical, and decontextualized structure.

Unlike Piagetians, who assume that only when a certain developmental level is achieved can conceptual learning start, Vygotskians propose that scientific learning itself promotes cognitive development. In order to start acquiring scientific concepts, of course, the child should have some experience with generalizations, which usually take the form of spontaneous, everyday concepts. Once the learning of scientific concepts gains momentum, however, it begins to exercise a reciprocal influence on everyday cognition. Scientific concepts move from the "top" downward—from verbal-logical formulae to concrete material. Spontaneous concepts move in the opposite direction, from the "bottom" upward—from contextual everyday experience to the formal structures of well-organized thought. "In working its slow way upwards, an everyday concept clears the path for a scientific concept in its downward development. It creates a series of structures necessary for the evolution of a concept's more primitive, elementary aspects, which gives it body and vitality. Scientific concepts, in turn, supply structures for the inward development of the child's spontaneous concepts toward consciousness and deliberate use" (Vygotsky, 1986, p. 194). The zone of proximal development (ZPD), mentioned earlier, can be conceptualized as a zone in which scientific concepts introduced by teachers interact with spontaneous concepts preexistent in children.

From the educational point of view the most interesting aspect of conceptual development is the dynamic of change in children's thought when exposed to scientific concepts. Instead of simply studying how the child's concepts change with age and at which point they become indistinguishable from those of adults, one may wish to undertake a dynamic analysis of what happens when scientific concepts, introduced by teachers, start to interact with spontaneous concepts held by children. This aspect was studied by Panofsky, John-Steiner, and Blackwell (1990) in their investigation of biological reasoning in fifth-grade students.

The study took place in a small rural school in New Mexico. Ranching, farming, hunting, and fishing were common experiences for many children in the class. The ethnic composition of the school was 75 percent Hispanic and 25 percent Anglo. All the children in the fifth grade were native English speakers, though some of them understood Spanish. The study took place during two months late in the school year.

Before the study began, children received explicit instruction in the principles of biological classification. In particular, instruction focused on the distinction between plants and animals, between vertebrates and invertebrates, and among such categories as mammal, reptile, amphibian, bird, and fish. Hierarchical relationships among these categories were also explained. The game Animal-Vegetable-Mineral played an important role in teaching categories. In order to succeed at this game, one must be able to use a hierarchical structure with nonoverlapping categories and to manipulate this structure in a logical and sequential way.

The study itself included two experimental activities: a set of concept-sorting tasks and a film-retelling task. The children were asked to perform three classification tasks, two in an initial session and one several weeks later. At the first session, the children were given a set of 20 pictures, 6 of plants and 14 of animals. They were asked to sort the pictures into two piles, to put each pile into an envelope, and to write on the envelope something that explained why these items "belonged together." During the second session, children were given the same pictures but with seven empty envelopes. Children were asked to sort the pictures into as many groups as they wanted, but no fewer than three. Several weeks later, the children were asked to sort 23 animal pictures into at least three groups. Pictures included 13 of the original group plus 10 new ones.

In the first task, 82 percent of the children separated the pictures taxonomically into plant and animal categories and labeled the envelopes accordingly. In the second and third tasks, which required a greater number of categories, the scientific grouping was much less pronounced: only 19 percent of the children used an exclusively taxonomic approach in the second task, and 25 percent in the third. Often children employed a combination of spontaneous and scientific principles in their sorting. For example, one of the students used the following grouping labels in the third task: birds, water animals, insects, animals that hunt, animals that are hunted. Everyday experience with hunting plus some ecological knowledge were here combined with taxonomic principles. In some children, the appropriate use of taxonomic categories was coexistent with a mixing of levels of abstraction. One of the children sorted pictures into the following categories in the third task: all birds, all fish, all insects, all reptiles, animals with backbones, animals without backbones, both amphibians. Some taxonomic labels were used in a pseudoscientific way, as when the label of reptiles was applied to both frog and earthworm because "They're all slimy." Obviously the perceptual feature here overpowered other possible criteria for inclusion.

From the results of the sorting tasks it became clear that the acquisition of scientific concepts in primary schoolchildren is indeed a complex interactive process. It is not an "all or nothing" switch from everyday to scientific conceptualization, but an intricate process that contains a number of intermediate stages further diversified by the specific cultural experiences of the children. The following aspects of the acquisition of taxonomic principles can be tentatively identified: (1) learning the distinction between everyday, ecological, and taxonomic categorization; (2)

learning different hierarchies within taxonomic categorization; (3) learning the principle of consistency of categorization. The authors of the study suggested that one way to advance children's understanding of these principles is to make classification systems an object of study: "Questions for investigation might include the organization of objects in space—such as how items are arranged in kitchens or workshops—and comparative analysis of different findings by peers investigating similar domains. Such investigations should lead to the development of active strategies for sorting or categorizing, which can be effectively applied as a system of discourse rather than as a rote fashion" (Panofsky, John-Steiner, and Blackwell, 1990, pp. 265–266). As will be discussed in Chapter 4, such an approach was realized by Feuerstein et al. (1980) in his mediated learning and Instrumental Enrichment program.

The second activity was the film-retelling task. The entire class viewed a fifteen-minute science film on different types of vision in animals. After a group discussion about the film, a representative subgroup of children participated in the experimental retelling task. The analysis of individual retellings suggested a correlation between recall and conceptional organization. Children who utilized taxonomic sorting strategies had the most extensive recall. They also recalled a greater portion of the taxonomic information contained in the film. The utterances of the children who used scientific concepts differed from others not only in quantity but also in quality. These speakers used strategies more characteristic of written language. They used a number of devices to achieve greater coherence in their narratives: explicit marking of topics, elaboration, transitions, and connectives. The use of such strategies implies that a speaker is able to plan both the form and the content of his or her speech.

The findings of the film-retelling experiment confirm Vygotsky's belief that the acquisition of scientific concepts has a reciprocal relationship with the acquisition of the higher-order forms of verbal discourse (Wertsch, 1985a). One may suggest that the same aspects of planning and awareness that are essential for conceptual activity are also realized in a child's discourse formation.

## Piaget and the Spirit of Progressive Education

Theoretical ideas frequently undergo considerable change in the course of their transition from the laboratory to the classroom. Piagetian ideas have been no exception. One of the most characteristic features of the assimilation of Piagetian ideas in the American educational system was the spirit of progressive education pervading it (Silberman, 1970).

Indeed, some of the older principles associated with progressive education turned out to be highly compatible with the Piagetian system. The principle of "learning by doing" could be easily translated into the Piagetian principle "from action to thought." The suggestion that the child is a true agent of his or her own learning was also characteristic of both traditions. Even the method of projects that featured so prominently in the progressive education tradition found a safe place within Piagetian-based learning programs (Wickens, 1973).

What is unmistakably Piagetian in such a hybrid system is the emphasis on the sequencing of curriculum material depending on the level of the child's cognitive development as established through Piagetian assessment procedures. For example, it is argued that the teaching of material requiring formal logical operations should be delayed until the necessary operations spontaneously appear in the child's reasoning. "We should try where possible, to teach children new concepts in the same order that these concepts emerge during spontaneous cognitive development" (Brainerd, 1978, p. 274).

Predictably, the infusion of Piagetian ideas into the American classroom produced mixed results. On the positive side one can mention the increased awareness on the part of educators of the role of reasoning in children's learning (Duckworth, 1987). The emphasis on independent discovery by children themselves helped a number of gifted students to reveal their true potential, abilities that could have been stymied by rote learning. Finally, the Piagetian approach stimulated interdisciplinary cooperation between cognitive psychologists and teachers. Teachers' attention was drawn to the fact that the methods of delivery of content material become effective only when the child's reasoning during the acquisition of this material is taken into account.

These positive aspects notwithstanding, there are serious doubts regarding the net effect of the popularity of Piagetian ideas, particularly when assimilated in a spirit of progressive education. A critique of education based on the Piagetian model appeared almost from the very beginning of its implementation in North American schools (Sullivan, 1967), but was not heeded at that time. One problematic point concerns the proliferation of thinking games at the expense of teaching verbal skills and content knowledge (Furth, 1970). Such thinking exercises are attractive for the child, but they often lack the systematicity provided by coherently presented content material. Attempts at teaching nonverbal thinking as a substitute for teaching language can, at their worst, result in such reading and writing backwardness that higher forms of learning are foreclosed (Modgil, Modgil, and Brown, 1983).

Another point of concern is the notion that learning should follow the course of development. In practice this leads to a delay in teaching science and certain types of mathematics until much later in school. The problem is that even at the age of fourteen, 75 percent of students consistently use concrete operations, and only 20 percent master formal operations (Shayer and Adey, 1981). This often necessitates special cognitive enrichment programs to prepare students for learning science. One may argue that this can be done much more efficiently and at an earlier age, if one accepts the Vygotskian position that education should lead development rather than follow it.

Piaget's equivocality regarding Vygotsky's distinction between "scientific" and "spontaneous" concepts translates into educational practices that do not prepare a child for genuine scientific reasoning, as opposed to everyday cognition. The attempt to move school closer to real-life tasks, which is another legacy of progressive education, often results in presenting real-life phenomena on a scriptlike, preconceptual level. As a consequence, when in the higher grades students are confronted by problems requiring scientific, conceptual reasoning they experience real shock, because nothing in their previous experience has prepared them for such a change of perspective.

Finally, and probably most important, the Piagetian notion that the child is a true agent of his or her learning fits well into the American cultural belief that education is primarily a way of revealing individual abilities and potentials. This belief leads to an overemphasis on individualized learning and a deemphasis on the issue of acquisition of knowledge as a group activity oriented toward specific sociocultural goals. One example may help to clarify this distinction. In a comparative analysis of mathematics teaching in American and Asian (Taiwanese and Japanese) schools it was shown that one of the apparently highly effective classroom activities employed by Asian educators is a group analysis of mistakes made by a specific student (Stigler and Perry, 1990). The student in question does not feel ashamed to be singled out, because the learning problem is not attributed to him or her as an individual, but rather serves as an example of what can go wrong in the learning process as such. In this context learning is understood as a process of acquisition of knowledge, skills, and concepts existent in culture, and not as a manifestation of individual abilities.

There is nothing wrong, of course, with an attempt to make education individualized. In the reality of the contemporary classroom, however, such an attitude often has negative consequences. The first is that only stronger and more highly motivated students benefit from being considered true agents of their own learning. The second problem lies in the fact that where learning is detached from sociocultural models, it becomes exceedingly difficult to agree on comprehensive educational requirements. In the following section I will focus on how these problems have been dealt with in the Vygotskian system.

## Vygotsky and Theoretical Learning

For many years Vygotskian theory developed exclusively in the Soviet Union. This circumstance cannot fail to leave a specific imprint on the theory's educational applications. The Soviet educational system has always presupposed a rather rigid set of comprehensive requirements, including a strong emphasis on the study of science, mathematics, and a standard list of classical works of Russian literature. At the same time, and for obvious political reasons, creativity, pluralism, and a critical approach in the social sciences were systematically discouraged. The highly centralized system of educational bureaucracy ensured that these requirements became truly comprehensive at least as a goal, if not as a reality. As a result special cultural-historical conditions favoring theoretical learning in ideologically neutral areas were created.

As mentioned earlier, Vygotsky drew an important distinction between scientific and spontaneous concepts. Spontaneous concepts originate in the child's everyday activity, while scientific concepts emerge from systematic school-based learning. Contemporary Vygotskians (Davydov, 1988a,b; Hedegaard, 1990) have further refined this distinction to include the differences between various types of school-based learning. They argue that in practice a considerable amount of school-based learning does not transcend the limits of empirical concept formation. Concepts acquired in this way differ from everyday concepts in the domain, but not in the method of acquisition and generation. The line should be drawn, therefore, between empirical and theoretical concepts. Empirical concepts are acquired through the identification of similar features in a group of concrete objects or observable phenomena and then labeling this feature with a verbal notion. For example, the notion of the circle is traditionally introduced in primary schools by demonstrating a number of round objects, such as a wheel, the sun, a pancake, and so on, and then explaining that a common feature of all these objects is their circular form. The principle of concept formation in this case is a simple abstraction that does not require any higher-level thinking and that can be achieved through habit formation.

Theoretical concepts have an essentially different nature. To understand an object or a process theoretically is to construct its ideal form and to be able to experiment with it. A paradigm of such experimentation is provided by the mental experiments carried out in classical science by Galileo, Descartes, and others. A theoretical concept is "generative" in the sense that it should be possible to generate from it a number of empirical outcomes, it is universal so that all empirical data are explainable through it, and it should not require the prior knowledge of all those phenomena it is expected to explain. For example, the theoretical definition of a circle (suggested by Spinoza) defines it as a figure produced by the rotation of a segment of a line with one free and one fixed end. Such a definition is generative because it provides a procedure for the generation of circles, it is universal because all possible circles can be generated in such a way, and it is theoretical because it requires no previous knowledge of round objects.

One may argue that there is little difference in introducing the notion of a circle to a child through the comparison of a number of round objects or through the manipulation of the rotating line; in both cases the child would most probably understand the meaning of a circle. The difference, however, is significant because in the first case the child would only learn how to distinguish round objects, while in the second case he or she would acquire a skill of theoretical comprehension. The first approach is product oriented, the second focuses on the process. This process helps the child to construct the essence of the object and thus liberates him or her from domination by the empirically given. The child starts to realize that essential characteristics of objects do not necessarily lie on the surface but should be uncovered. This is an important lesson for understanding scientific truth, where the lack of coincidence between empirical appearance and theoretical essence is the norm, and not an exception.

When designing a program based on the principles of theoretical learning, the teacher should start with the most general definition of the problem so that the relationships central to this problem are revealed. In a traditional primary school nature class, for example, students usually acquire interesting but often disjointed information about various physical and biological phenomena. In the framework of a theoretical learning program the teacher always first formulates some central scientific problem. For the nature class, the teacher may choose the problem of the contradictory relationships between an organism and the environment. The teacher then assists students in formulating the model that serves as a conceptual tool for exploring the learning material. Such a model includes three main elements: organism, population, and environment. In the next step all possible relationships between the elements of the model are explored. New problems and tasks stemming from the model are generated. The learning process involves what Hedegaard (1990) calls a "double move": the teacher guarantees that the theoretical model is used by children as a conceptual tool, while children are encouraged to observe and manipulate with concrete manifestations of the principles embodied in the model. Through trips to natural history museums, through films, and through textbook material, students learn about the lifestyle of specific animals, their habitats, and the structure of their group life. Then students "map" the empirical data onto the model. The model itself becomes transformed to account for new types of relationships. As a result students learn about ways of survival, cohabitation of different species, variation, and selection, all within the scientific concept of biological evolution.

Another important aspect of learning explored by Vygotskians relates to the value attached by students to different types of activity. For example, Elkonin (1971) maintains that the failure to teach scientific concepts to young adolescents often stems from the wrong premise that learning activity per se has a high value for this age group. He further argues that it is group activity and the establishment of personal relationships that has the highest priority for young adolescents. In the traditional classroom, based on the teacher's narrative and students' individual work, the lack of recognition of this priority leads to serious problems. The teacher has a hard time keeping students' attention, because in the classroom the students are engaged in a "parallel activity" focused on nonacademic problems of an interpersonal nature. Vygotskians suggest turning this "obstacle" into the motor of learning. This can be achieved through the organization of class work according to the principle of collectively distributed problem solving. The essence of this approach is in presenting the task not for individuals but for the whole class. The task is presented in such a way that several groups of students are responsible for different segments of problem solving. The final result can be achieved only when all partial solutions are integrated. The partial results become compatible, however, only when all students are using the same theoretical approach and the same model for the representation of essential relationships. Thus the students' desire to engage in interpersonal contact becomes fully realized, but it is employed as a means for achieving the goals of learning.

The role of a teacher also changes in this context. Instead of appearing as an authoritarian figure who can change the course of the lesson at will, the teacher becomes a senior member of the "scientific group." The teacher's role is that of advisor and participant. The character of the involvement is now dictated by the logic of problem solving itself. This change in the teacher's role not only leads to more relaxed teacher-student relationships, but also serves as an important model of the distribution of functions within the group engaged in problem solving. This fits well into Vygotsky's (1978) understanding of the process of activity internalization. According to Vygotsky, many relations that first appear in a real group activity are later internalized by the student as the relations between his or her inner intellectual processes. Thus the role of a teacher as an expert and advisor working within the group becomes internalized by the child as his own internal function of reference and control.

As already noted, the emergence of theoretical learning programs in the Soviet Union was facilitated by the specific cultural-historical context. One should be aware of these contexts when planning the implementation of theoretical learning programs in other countries.

First, the Soviet theoretical learning programs took for granted the existence of a wide social consensus regarding the ultimate goals of education. It was supposed that society as a whole expects its children to appreciate classical literature on the one hand, and to prepare themselves for careers in modern science and technology on the other. In a society with many divergent and often antagonistic subcultures this presumption may well be groundless. The task of an American educator, therefore, is more difficult. The educator must simultaneously demonstrate the value of verbal and scientific literacy in modern society and introduce students to the theoretical methods of acquiring this literacy.

Second, by focusing on physics, mathematics, and language, the advocates of theoretical learning largely neglected the social and political sciences. Even for scholars, these subjects are difficult to present in a theoretically coherent form. The task confronting psychologists and educators is twofold, that is, to develop theoretical learning models for the social sciences and to elaborate the relationship between these models and social knowledge that resists scientific conceptualization.

Third, the model of different activities for different age groups (Elkonin, 1971) was developed with a certain sociocultural framework in mind. Yet this model also appears to contain certain universal features, since in some instances it closely resembles Erikson's (1963) psychosocial stages theory. Only further research and application of this model can determine the degree of its universality and those adjustments that should be done to make it work for the diverse populations of students.

All in all, the educational application of Vygotskian ideas teaches us that psychological theories can be neither value free nor culturally neutral. When proposing an explanation of the child's learning processes or suggesting methods for their enhancement we cannot escape the questions about the cultural and societal goals this learning strives to achieve.

# 3 ⤳

# *The Mediated Learning Experience and Psychological Tools*

Despite its significant contribution to the cognitive reorientation of psychology and education, Piagetian theory, as we have seen, leaves many questions either unanswered or answered in ways that are not entirely satisfactory. There are two major problems with the Piagetian cognitive approach. First, the sociocultural aspect of learning remains largely beyond the scope of Piaget's theory. Second, the learning process that Piaget proposed occurred as a direct interaction of the child with the environment. Human mediators were largely excluded from the exchange.

Alternative theoretical approaches have been proposed by Lev Vygotsky and Reuven Feuerstein. Vygotsky focused his attention on the sociocultural mediation of the learning process. For him the learning process appears first as a process of appropriation by the child of the methods of action existent in a given culture. In such an appropriation, symbolic tools play a crucial role. Feuerstein, an Israeli psychologist and educator, focused on the role of the human mediator in the interaction between the child and the environment and suggested a radical dichotomy between direct and mediated learning (Feuerstein, Rand, and Hoffman, 1979; Feuerstein et al., 1980; Feuerstein, 1990).

## Direct Learning versus Mediated Learning

In direct learning, the child interacts with the environment. This interaction can take the form of observational learning, trial and error, conditioning, or other activities in which the child interacts with stimuli directly. In a mediated learning situation, an adult or more competent peer places him- or herself "between" the environment and the child—thus radically changing the conditions of the interaction. The mediator selects, changes, amplifies, and interprets objects and processes to the child.

The concept of mediated learning changes our view of both animal and human behavior. Let us consider, for example, how children or young animals learn to avoid dangerous objects. According to the classical, behaviorist paradigm, learning must include a number of direct exposures of the child to a dangerous stimulus (for example, a hot object), which in due time results in the formation of a conditional avoidance reflex. But this mechanism, which can be studied in animals under experimental laboratory conditions, seems to have a very low ecological validity. Ethological studies suggest that avoidance of harmful stimuli is achieved in quite a different way (Bronson, 1968). Young animals tend to avoid all objects that have not previously been encountered in the presence of their mother. Learning, therefore, is achieved not through direct exposure, but through the indirect experience mediated by the presence (or absence) of the mother.

The role of mediation becomes even more pronounced in human learning. For example, aside from cases of severe sociocultural deprivation, the human child does not learn about harmful stimuli through direct exposure. Instead a complex process of mediated learning takes place, in which the parents or other caretakers insert themselves "between" the stimuli and the child. The caretaker indicates to the child which objects are dangerous. Sometimes the caretaker deliberately exposes a child to a dangerous or unpleasant stimulus under controlled conditions, creating the equivalent of a psychological "vaccination." The caretaker explains to the child the meaning of dangerous situations. Finally, the caretaker stimulates generalization, creating in the child the notion of a dangerous situation and a possible response to it.

This example suggests that there is a qualitative difference between learning based on direct exposure to stimuli and learning mediated by another human being. Since the notion of mediation began well before either Vygotsky's or Feuerstein's theories, it is relevant to discuss briefly the history of philosophical and sociological theories of mediated interaction.

## Mediated Interaction: Philosophical and Sociological Aspects

On the philosophical plane, the notion of mediation *(Vermittlung)* constitutes one of the cornerstones of the Hegelian system (Kojeve, 1986). Both directly and indirectly, particularly through Marx, this notion influenced Vygotsky's approach and the theories of his followers, including Leontiev (1978) and Luria (1976).

According to Hegel, the very existence of human-type activity depends on the transition from the immediate, animal-type activity of satisfaction of needs, which coincides with the ability of the individual animal, to the human satisfaction of needs dependent on the activity of others. Human beings satisfy their needs indirectly through work with end products, which are intended not for the producer but for others. "The being that acts to satisfy its *own* instincts, which—as such—are always natural, does not rise above Nature: it remains a natural being, an animal. But by acting to satisfy an instinct that is *not* my own, I am acting in relation to what is not—for me—instinct. I am acting in relation to an idea, a nonbiological end" (Kojeve, 1986, p. 42).

Hegel links the emergence of human consciousness and self-consciousness to this process of mediated activity—which is work. The philosophical notion of mediation already suggests a whole range of possible mediating agents. First, work presupposes material tools interposed between the human individual and the natural object. These tools, though directed at natural objects, also have a reciprocal influence on the individual, thus changing his or her type of activity and cognition. Second, because work is always work for somebody else, then the social and psychological characteristics of the other person enter the equation. Finally, because work is impossible without symbolic representations, these symbols and the means of their transmission become two additional mediatory agents.

Now let us turn to the sociological plane. Here the issue of mediatory mechanisms embedded in the structure of human society was raised early on by G. H. Mead (1974). Mead made an important distinction between stimuli and objects: instead of just perceiving and responding to stimuli, human beings interact with objects. Unlike stimuli, objects are not given: they are "constructed." The "construction" of objects becomes possible only because stimuli of the environment take on cer-

tain meanings in the course of human activity, which is social in its
nature.

> The meaning of a thing for a person grows out of the ways in
> which other persons act toward the person with regard to the
> thing . . . Their actions operate to define the thing for the per-
> son. Thus, symbolic interactionism sees meanings as social
> products, as creations that are formed in and through the
> defining activities of people as they interact. (Blumer, 1969,
> pp. 4–5)

The interaction between the individual and the environment is never
immediate; it is always mediated by meanings that originate "outside"
the individual—in the world of social relations. Moreover, unlike animals, human beings are capable of becoming objects to themselves. Thus
an essential feature of human cognition is that it is based on the internalized form of what originally appeared as social interactions.

## Vygotsky's Theory of Mediated Activity

Vygotsky (1978, 1986) proposed that higher mental processes be considered as functions of mediated activity. He suggested three major classes
of mediators: material tools, "psychological tools," and other human
beings (see Kozulin, 1990a). Material tools have only an indirect
influence on human psychological processes, because they are directed
at processes in nature. Nevertheless, the use of material tools puts new
demands on human mental processes. Vygotsky suggested that the historical progress of tool-mediated activity from primitive to more advanced forms should be taken into account in a study of comparative
human cognition (Vygotsky and Luria, 1993).

According to Vygotsky, material tools do not exist as individual
implements; they presuppose collective use, interpersonal communication, and symbolic representation. This symbolic aspect of the tool-mediated activity gives rise to a new and important class of mediators that
Vygotsky designated "psychological tools." While material tools are directed at the objects of nature, psychological tools mediate humans' own
psychological processes. Among the most ancient psychological tools
Vygotsky mentioned are such "psychological fossils" as "casting lots,

tying knots, and counting fingers" (1978, p. 127). Casting lots appears in a situation where the uncertainty of making a decision, caused by the presence of two equipotent and opposing stimuli, is resolved by the application of an artificial and arbitrary stimulus—dice aimed at the subject's own psychological processes. Tying knots exemplifies the introduction of an elementary external mnemonic device to ensure the retrieval of information from memory. Finger counting is the adaptation of an always-available "tool" for the organization of higher mental processes involved in elementary arithmetic operations. Beyond these primitive "tools" lies the vast area of higher-order symbolic mediators, which include natural and artificial languages as well as discourses and cultural-symbolic systems of different epochs and nations. One of the major goals of Vygotsky's theory was to develop a typology of higher mental processes that would reflect the historical transition from one system of psychological tools to another (Vygotsky and Luria, 1993). An empirical study of such a transition and its psychological consequences was undertaken in the early 1930s by Vygotsky and Luria in the context of cultural change in Soviet Central Asia (Luria, 1976).

Regarding mediation through another individual, Vygotsky suggested two possible approaches. The first was expressed in the famous statement that "every function in the child's cultural development appears twice: first, on the social level, and later on the individual level, first, *between* people *(interpsychological),* and then *inside* the child *(intrapsychological)*" (Vygotsky, 1978, p. 57). As an illustration Vygotsky cited the phenomenon that was first noticed by J. M. Baldwin and later investigated by Piaget, namely, that a child's ability to consider different points of view on the mental plane depends on actual arguments between children. More recently this phenomenon has been discussed by Doise and Mugny (1984) and Tudge (1990).

The second approach focuses on the role of the other individual as a mediator of meaning. An illustrative example of this is the development of indicatory gesticulation in the child. According to Vygotsky, gesture first appears as a natural attempt to grasp an object. The grasping movement is interpreted by an adult as gesture; thus the human meaning of the natural act is supplied by the adult to the child from the "outside." Accordingly, the address of the movement changes from that of the object to that of a human subject. Movement itself becomes transformed and reduced—it "starts" as a grasping attempt and becomes a real gesture. Later, such gestures are internalized and become the child's inner commands to him- or herself. The meaning of one's own activity is thus formed by mediation through another individual. Vygotsky believed that this principle held for the whole personality as well: "One may say that only through the other do we become ourselves; this rule applies to each psychological function as well as to the personality as a whole" (1983, p. 144).

For the purpose of the present discussion, it is important to emphasize that mediation through another individual was closely linked in Vygotsky's theory to the notion of symbolic function. The human mediator appeared first as a carrier of signs, symbols, and meanings. No attempt was made by Vygotsky to elaborate the activities of human mediators beyond their function as vehicles of symbolic tools, which left considerable lacunae in his theory of mediation. These lacunae, as we shall see, were filled by the work of Feuerstein and his colleagues. In the process, the entire issue of mediated learning appeared in a new light.

## Mediated Learning Experience

Mediated learning experience (MLE) theory is the product of several decades of clinical and educational work (Feuerstein, Rand, and Hoffman, 1979; Feuerstein et al., 1980; Feuerstein, Rand, and Rynders, 1988; Feuerstein, 1990). This has included observations of and work with culturally different groups, culturally deprived individuals, and learning disabled and mentally handicapped children and adolescents. The central question that MLE theory attempts to answer is: what is the cause of individual differences in cognitive development? Usually this question is conceptualized through the notion of relative contributions of the organism and the environment (Bronfenbrenner, 1979). These contributions are assumed to directly affect cognitive development and lead to different outcomes. Clinical and educational practice, however, provides endless examples of cognitive developmental outcomes that cannot be explained on the basis of this model (Gallagher and Ramey, 1987). The same form of cognitive deficiency is often associated with quite different sets of organismic/environmental factors, while apparently similar organismic/environmental combinations often lead to significantly different cognitive-developmental outcomes ranging from normal to pathological. This paradox can be resolved if we accept the existence of the proximal factor, which can moderate the effect of organismic and environmental factors. MLE theory suggests that organismic and environmental factors constitute only *distal* determinants of cognitive development, while mediated learning experience (or the lack of it) constitutes the *proximal* determinant. The effect of distal determinants on cognitive development occurs primarily through their influence on MLE. This implies that one and the same combination of distal factors can be associated with a different type of cognitive development, depending on what happens on the MLE level. This hypothesis has been tested in respect to different proximal factors, including determinants as strong as birth weight (Klein, Weider, and Greenspan, 1987).

What, then, is MLE? MLE is a special quality of mediated interaction between the child and environmental stimuli. This quality is achieved by the interposition of an initiated and intentioned adult "between" the stimuli of the environment and the child. The interaction becomes mediated if certain criteria, to be discussed later, are met. (MLE is important for adult learning as well, but for the purposes of this discussion we focus on issues of MLE in children and adolescents.)

Earlier we discussed how children learn about dangerous objects. An essential element of such learning is the mediation provided by the adult who indicates dangerous objects, explains their meaning, undertakes psychological "vaccination," and so on. The ultimate goal of mediated learning is to make the child sensitive to learning through direct exposure to stimuli and to develop in the child cognitive prerequisites for such direct learning.

MLE not only differs in principle from the experience of direct learning, but also differs from nonmediating types of interaction. Not every interaction involving a child, an adult, and an object leads to MLE. To distinguish MLE from other interactive experiences a number of criteria have been elaborated (Feuerstein, 1990).

## Intentionality/Reciprocity

The major contribution of the mediating adult is to turn the interactive situation from an incidental into an intentional experience. This intentionality has two foci: one is the object, the other is the child. Some characteristics of the object—such as its location, brightness, and arrangement of its parts—are "transformed" by the adult so that the object is thereby experienced and not merely passively registered by the child. These physical transformations are accompanied by direct statements affirming the intentionality of the adult, for example, "I want you to see this; therefore I made it bigger," or "I want you to see how it appears; so I will show it to you twice." In a more general sense, intentionality transforms any interactive situation from accidental into purposeful. The adult ceases to be a mere provider of objects, information, or verbal orders, and becomes a source of constant affirmation that the objects and/or information involved are indeed intended for the child.

At the same time, it is not the object per se but the child's cognitive processes that are the primary target of mediated interaction, and this, too, should be made clear to the child. In a learning situation, the child should realize that the real objective of learning activity is not a particular task or a puzzle but the child's own thinking. By constantly focusing on the child's state of attention, problem-solving strategies, mistakes, and insights, the adult infuses the learning situation with a sense of purpose and intentionality. As a result, all three participants in the interactive situation become transformed: the object loses its natural form, becoming an educational construct; the child acquires MLE; and the adult acquires experience as a mediator.

### Transcendence

While in the case of direct learning one can only hope that it somehow affects cognition beyond the immediately present task, in the mediated experience the transcendent character of learning becomes one of its most important features. Whatever the specific subject of MLE may be, it is this transcendence into something else that gives MLE its particular quality. For example, a child's feeding during a fixed time period has a "surface" value of providing a child with nourishment and, possibly, teaching him or her the sensory-motor skill of manipulating a spoon; the same activity, however, may have the transcendent value of teaching the child the notion of time, schedule, recurrence of similar events, and so on.

The above examples point to one particularly important aspect of transcendent mediation: to be effective it need not necessarily be either conscious or deliberate. Many parents skillfully employ mediating techniques leading to transcendence without ever being aware of them. This brings us to the issue of the transmission of culture. The transmission of culture from generation to generation often takes a ritualized form, with participants following a traditional "script" that does not require much ingenuity. Many of these "scripts"—such as the one recited on the first night of Passover—contain numerous mediational devices. The very meaning of Passover is to provide a transcending link between the "surface script" of the family gathering, around the festive table, and the "deep script" of Jewish history and experience anchored in the exodus from Egypt. Such links are culturally important to every people.

## Meaning

The example of Passover, together with the issue of transcendence, brings forth the third criterion, that of meaning. MLE becomes possible only when stimuli, events, or information are infused with meaning by the mediator. It is possible for a child to sit through the entire Passover service and gain no mediated experience at all, if the adults fail to conduct the event in a mutually meaningful way. This shows how even the richest of rituals can lose its mediational value. Once an event becomes a mere sequence of strange, behavioral acts—devoid of purpose and affective investment, the situation loses its mediational potential. That is why MLE theory is incompatible with certain behaviorist principles and practices that leave meaning beyond the sphere of psychological analysis and modification.

Intentionality, transcendence, and meaning constitute the basic, necessary parameters of any MLE interaction. Other parameters, such as the mediation of a feeling of competence, or the mediation of a challenge, may vary depending on the task or the cultural background of the individual. (For a full list of MLE parameters, see Feuerstein, 1990.)

## Lack of MLE

The MLE theory was not conceived of as a psychological theory of normal development, but emerged from a multitude of clinical and educational data on the behavior and thinking of retarded performers (for illustrative case studies, see Feuerstein, Rand, and Rynders, 1988). For this reason, the role of MLE was first defined through negative examples—those cases when a child's performance was deficient owing to the lack or insufficiency of mediation.

There are two major causes for a lack of MLE: an insufficient amount of mediation, and those conditions that render a normal amount or type of mediation insufficient or inadequate. The absence of actual mediation is particularly characteristic of cases where, upon careful examination, organic or hereditary precursors of retarded performance can be ruled out. In its pure form, the lack of mediation is observed in children whose parents and other caretakers do not extend their attention beyond the here-and-now satisfaction of the children's vital needs. Children are fed, clothed, and warned of imminent danger, but they are left without the mediated experience required for the formation of the cognitive prerequisites necessary for the development of higher-level psychological functions (see Sewell and Price, 1991). As a result, children grow up with what Feuerstein has called an "episodic grasp of reality." Separate experiences, linked only to specific stimuli or reinforcers, remain unconnected in the child's mind. Behind the episodic grasp of reality lies an underdevelopment of such learning prerequisites as spontaneous comparative behavior, planning, hypothetical reasoning, formation of representations, and other cognitive processes.

The question may immediately arise whether the observed retarded performances were indeed caused by the lack of MLE or were the result of direct organic and/or environmental factors. The answer to this question lies in the body of research dedicated to the dynamic methods of assessment and rehabilitation that include mediation as their essential component (Feuerstein, Rand, and Hoffman, 1979; Lidz, 1987a; Haywood and Tzuriel, 1992). In simple terms, the dynamic assessment technique includes intensive mediational investment between the pre- and post-test. If such an investment results in a considerable improvement of performance, as compared with standard tests and nonmediational instruction, then there are ample grounds to maintain that the lack of MLE was the original culprit. In the course of work by multiple researchers, the concept of dynamic cognitive assessment was proposed more or less independently by the followers of Vygotsky and by Feuerstein and his colleagues.

## The Zone of Proximal Development and
## Dynamic Cognitive Assessment

Vygotsky's innovative approach to psychological functions carried with it the possibility of an alternative approach to their assessment (Vygotsky, 1986; Minick, 1987; Lidz, 1995). He was one of the first critics of IQ testing. According to Vygotsky cognitive ability is not a "natural" entity but a sociocultural construct that emerges from the child's interaction with the environment. The subject of ability, therefore, is not the child alone but a pair: child–culture. The development of abilities is also perceived not as a natural process of maturation and the acquisition of new information, but rather as an increasing ability to apply new cultural tools to one's own psychological processes.

The issue of assessment appeared in Vygotsky's (1986) theory in the context of the so-called zone of proximal development (ZPD). Vygotsky argued that the task of assessment must identify not only those cognitive processes of the child that are fully developed, but also those that are in a state of being developed at the time of assessment. This development, according to Vygotsky, depends on a cooperative interaction between the child and the adult, who represents the culture and assists the child in acquiring the necessary symbolic tools of learning. For this reason, the emergent cognitive functions can be identified through the incorporation of cooperative learning into the assessment procedure. The difference in the results of performance with and without help indicates the ZPD. The ZPD can be interpreted both qualitatively and quantitatively. Qualitatively it points to those cognitive functions that are absent in the unaided performance of the child, but reveal themselves when the child is aided by adults. Quantitatively the ZPD is a measure of the difference between unaided and aided performance. ZPD may also be interpreted as reflecting the ability of the child to benefit from adult assistance and cooperative learning. For this reason the establishment of the ZPD in the child is an important task of education. The child with a narrow ZPD may have a poor prospect in terms of his or her ability to benefit from the instruction provided by adults.

For a variety of social and political reasons, cognitive assessment based on the principles of ZPD has not been systematically developed in the Soviet Union or modern-day Russia. Although some elements of this approach were used by Luria (1979) and his colleagues in the field of neuropsychology and special education, true appreciation of ZPD as a guiding principle for cognitive assessment appeared in the context of more recent critiques of IQ testing. For the most part these critiques were of two kinds. The first focused on the faulty and/or discriminatory nature of any intellectual/cognitive testing and called for its outright abolition. The second critique focused on technical problems and suggested some improvements without changing the underlying paradigm of the standard psychometric approach.

More recently a number of attempts have been made to venture beyond both the total rejection and the complete acceptance of the psychometric paradigm. These alternative approaches have been developed in the context of different research and evaluation traditions and in some instances reflected conflicting goals and objectives. Against such a background, it is useful to inquire into those tacit assumptions that constitute the paradigm of standard intellectual testing:

1. The manifest level of functioning reveals the child's inner abilities more or less accurately.
2. Unaided performance is the best format for assessment.
3. The goal of testing is to predict the future functioning and to classify the child according to his or her level of abilities.

The emergence of dynamic cognitive assessment is associated with the revision of these tacit assumptions and the development of an alternative set of principles:

1. Cognitive processes are highly modifiable. For this reason the task of assessment is to ascertain the degree of modifiability, rather than the manifest level of functioning.
2. Interactive assessment that includes the learning phase provides a better insight into the child's learning capacities than unaided performance.
3. The goal of assessment is to reveal the child's learning potential and to suggest psychoeducational interventions aimed at the enhancement and realization of this potential.

Research and development of the methods of cognitive assessment based on the notion of ZPD were called upon to answer a number of questions associated with the new dynamic paradigm. One of them is a question of qualitative versus quantitative interpretation of ZPD. Should one focus on the quantitative difference between the child's pre- and postintervention performance, or should the emphasis be placed on the qualitative, structural changes in the child's responses? The second important question is how to operationalize the aid provided by adults. The third question seeks to determine the goal of dynamic assessment. Should it include some prediction regarding the child's future performance or should it focus only on psychoeducational recommendations aimed at the optimal development of the child's learning potential?

The quantitative approach to ZPD is best represented by the work of Campione and Brown (1987). The authors suggested studying the amount of help needed for a child to attain the criterion level of performance, rather than an increase in the child's performance itself. The choice of the task domain was guided by the idea of selecting such domains where rules and principles can be learned by the child and applied to novel types of problems; in this way both learning and transfer processes can be studied. The aim of producing solid quantitative data compelled the authors to make the procedure task- rather than child-oriented. For that reason the help given to the child took the form of a fixed sequence of hints. The initial hints were very general, with subsequent ones becoming more and more specific. The last "hint" actually provided a detailed instruction for generating the correct answer.

One of the central findings made by the authors was that learning and transfer scores are not only related to standard ability measures, but also provide additional information not captured by the standard tests. In two experiments, one using the simplified version of Raven's Progressive Matrices and the other using the letter series completion task, it was shown that while the pretest ability score accounted for 60 percent of the post-test-gain score variance, learning and transfer scores still accounted for significant additional portions of the variance in gain scores (22 percent for learning and 17 percent for transfer scores).

In particular, the issue of far-transfer (that is, the ability of the child to apply a learned rule to new material) came to the forefront. While learning and maintenance of the rule sometimes failed to distinguish between more and less successful students, the far-transfer task made this distinction very clear. This finding has a significant educational implication. It is not sufficient to plan instruction in such a way that rules and principles are learned; it is probably more important to develop students' ability to combine these rules and apply them to novel material.

In Europe, ZPD-based assessment is associated with so-called learning tests (Guthke, 1993; Guthke and Wingenfeld, 1992). There are two major types of learning tests: short term and long term. A short-term learning test requires just one session, during which the child is given a task (for example, Raven's Colored Progressive Matrices) and immediate feedback. The amount of feedback ranges from simple correct/incorrect comments to more substantial help, including the puzzle form of the matrices with which the child can try to solve problems again and again. The long-term test requires a number of days for its administration. Students are presented with a pretest that includes verbal analogies and numerical and figural sequences. Following the pretest students receive programmed instruction manuals and are taught metacognitive strategies for solving the test items. After the instructional phase students are presented with the parallel post-test.

Research on learning tests confirms that post-test gains cannot be fully predicted from the pretest, and that, therefore, the instructional effects provide additional diagnostic information regarding the students' learning abilities. Longitudinal studies show that while for average intelligence children the predictive validity of the learning tests was not significantly better than that of the standard tests, this was not true for the more problematic children. Using Raven's Colored Progressive Matrices Test and Sequence of Sets Test, Guthke and Wingenfeld (1992) were able to demonstrate that for children with below-average intelligence the predictive validity coefficients were significantly higher for the learning tests when compared with the conventional static tests. Learning tests seem to be particularly informative when used with learning disabled, handicapped, or educationally deprived children.

These applications of the ZPD principle to cognitive assessment strengthened the quantitative aspect and the uniformity of the dynamic assessment procedure. At the same time Vygotsky's concern with child-oriented qualitative evaluation did not find its proper expression here. There is a certain irony in the fact that this later aspect found its full realization in Feuerstein's learning potential assessment approach, which was developed independently and without direct relation to Vygotsky's theory (Feuerstein, Rand, and Hoffman, 1979).

## The Learning Potential Assessment Device

The aim of the learning potential assessment device (LPAD) is to produce structural changes in the child's cognitive functioning and to explore the necessary conditions for further changes (Feuerstein, Rand, and Hoffman, 1979). For this reason, the LPAD procedure involves intensive dynamic interaction among three components: the task, the child, and the examiner. Using the MLE technique, the examiner attempts to correct the deficient cognitive functions of the child. Performance of LPAD tasks can be scored, but it is not the aim of LPAD procedure to produce a total score that would classify a child in any standardized way. The result of LPAD assessment is a descriptive profile of modifiability that registers the domain in which changes have occurred, the quality, generality, and permanence of the achieved change, and the nature and amount of intervention required for structural modification. The ultimate result of LPAD assessment is a prescriptive psychoeducational recommendation.

The LPAD battery includes tasks addressing perceptual, memory, problem-solving, and metacognitive processes. Some of these tasks (for example, Raven's Standard Progressive Matrices or the Rey-Osterreith Figure Copying Test) are used elsewhere in their static form; others (for example, Set Variations I and II) have been developed specifically for the LPAD. There is no time limit for LPAD task performance, but speed and tempo of performance are registered. The time of the complete assessment varies widely depending on the severity of the condition and the amount of mediation.

LPAD research literature includes three types of data: single case studies; application to individuals with special needs (for example, deaf students); and evaluation of the effectiveness of the group administration of LPAD.

Single case studies typically focus on severely handicapped children whose prognosis based on standard IQ measures was quite pessimistic. The LPAD assessment not only reveals the hidden learning potential of these children, but also reorients their parents and teachers from passive acceptance to active modification. In a few cases where standard measures predicted permanent mental retardation, children assessed by LPAD eventually succeeded in mastering a regular school curriculum and became independent, working individuals (Feuerstein, Rand, and Rynders, 1988).

Special needs studies (for example, deaf students, immigrants, prison inmates) focus on revealing learning abilities which for a variety of reasons, including deafness, poor understanding of language, and educational deprivation, fail to manifest themselves under ordinary circumstances. It was shown that deaf students significantly improved their performance in the Kohs Block Design task as a consequence of being exposed to LPAD assessment (Keane, Tannenbaum, and Kraft, 1992). Even a short LPAD intervention can substantially improve the standard test performance of the educationally deprived individual. In a study of a group of prison inmates with an educational mean grade level of 3.9 years the subjects' cognitive modifiability was measured by the difference in their pre- and post-test scores on the Lorge-Thorndike Nonverbal Intelligence Test, administered in a standard fashion. LPAD assessment served as an intervention program. Significant improvement was reported in the subjects' Lorge-Thorndike scores so that in the post-test they did not differ from those of a parallel group of inmates whose educational level was grade 8 or higher (Silverman and Waksman, 1992).

Group administration of LPAD differs from the individual one in that mediation is carried out for a group as a whole. Such a group administration often serves as a preliminary screening procedure for identifying less successful students who should then be brought in for individual LPAD. The screening use of group LPAD is of particular help when the group in question is composed of individuals who have never before experienced testing or a formal learning situation (for example, refugees from third world countries). Apart from its use with an initial screening group, LPAD can be used as an indicator of the average learning potential and specific cognitive deficiencies of a given group in addition to serving as a tool for exploring those conditions under which children's cognitive functioning is modified in the most effective way. For example, the intensity of mediation during the learning phase of LPAD turned out to be an important variable. It was shown that while average and above-average students benefit from even low-intensity mediation, their less advanced peers can attain spectacular achievements only under conditions of intensive mediation (Tzuriel and Feuerstein, 1992).

Dynamic cognitive assessment, particularly Feuerstein's version, offers a new philosophy and technique of psychoeducational testing.

This philosophy is based on the belief in human cognitive modifiability and the goal of shaping the testing situation to answer prospective rather than retrospective questions. Assessment according to this approach should be able to provide the answers to the question of how to change the condition—rather than the question of what caused this condition or its severity. The increase in the child's cognitive modifiability in the process of assessment is the pivotal element of this approach. The principles of dynamic cognitive assessment call for the reevaluation of relationships between psychologists-diagnosticians on the one hand and educators on the other. Psychologists should incorporate the goals of educational intervention into the body of their assessment and report writing; educators should pay greater attention to those modifiable cognitive processes that serve as prerequisites for students' content learning.

## Cultural Difference and Cultural Deprivation

On the sociocultural level, the lack of mediation is often associated with the rejection or breakdown of the system of cultural transmission. The influence of this condition on the child is twofold. The child becomes deprived of those devices of mediated learning that were incorporated into the traditional cultural schemas and rituals of his or her parents. At the same time, parents themselves often abandon or are forced to revoke their prerogative as mediators because their old culture is perceived as irrelevant, while the new culture is not yet mastered. As a result, the child is left to confront the world on a "here-and-now" basis without the help of the transcending devices of the cultural-historical tradition.

Feuerstein (1991) observed that the process of adaptation of an immigrant group to a new culture depends more on the group's ability to preserve cultural transmission under the new conditions rather than on the "distance" between the original and the new culture. Although the content of the original culture and the methods of transmission may be very different from those accepted in the dominant culture, what is important is that the individual has an experience of cultural learning and a strong feeling of cultural identity. For example, at the time of their immigration, Yemenite Jews represented a group that was quite distant and different from the Israeli culture into which they were introduced in a dramatic and sudden manner. Yet the changes that this group undertook in adapting to the dominant culture and their overall social achievements are more impressive than those of some other immigrant groups whose original educational systems were closer to European standards and who had greater exposure to modern technology. Although more "advanced" in terms of distal socioeconomic conditions, these groups suffered from the consequences of cultural deprivation. Their reduced modifiability, therefore, was the result of insufficient MLE on the proximal level, rather than of cultural difference.

Feuerstein made no special reference to deficient cognitive functions characteristic of cultural deprivation as opposed to cultural difference. The criterion of differentiation between these two conditions lies primarily in the potential for modifiability, which, he maintains, is low in culturally deprived persons. A culturally different individual may manifest certain "deficient" cognitive functions, but is expected to overcome them relatively quickly. One may notice that, although higher-order symbolic tools are not mentioned in Feuerstein's theoretical discussion, his applied system of Instrumental Enrichment (Feuerstein et al., 1980) includes just such entities as major tools for the remediation of deficient cognitive functions. One may thus conclude that, at least implicitly, the acquisition of higher-order symbolic tools is perceived by Feuerstein as a necessary condition for the enhancement of learning abilities.

From Vygotsky's point of view cultural difference is associated with the presence of an alternative system of psychological tools leading to the specific development of cultural psychological functions—for example, memory mediated by an oral tradition instead of written records (Vygotsky and Luria, 1993).

## The Matrix of Interaction between MLE and Psychological Tools

The above discussion allows us to formulate an integrative model that includes both the MLE and higher-order psychological tools such as writing, numerical, and other abstract notational systems. I propose the following four-fold matrix of interaction between MLE and psychological tools:

A. Positive MLE/Tools available;
B. Positive MLE/Tools unavailable;

C. Deficient MLE/Tools available;

D. Deficient MLE/Tools unavailable.

Condition A is characteristic of the normal cognitive development of the child who has acquired and successfully internalized such higher-order psychological tools as written language and the numerical system. It is important to emphasize here that psychological tools should not only be available to the child, but should be properly mediated to him or her. This includes the ability to read for meaning and to understand mathematical problem solving rather than mechanically performing arithmetic operations.

Condition B is characteristic of a culturally different individual who received a sufficient MLE in his or her native culture, but who was neither exposed to nor provided with the mediation of higher-order psychological tools. The prototypical case of this kind will be a child reared in a nonliterate traditional culture which, at the same time, cultivates its own well-articulated means of cultural transmission. The child in question is supposed to have the general prerequisites for learning, including articulated perception, spontaneous comparative behavior, the ability to formulate and test hypotheses, nonegocentric response modalities, and other cognitive functions as listed by Feuerstein (1990).

There is no agreement among researchers regarding whether all the necessary cognitive prerequisites can be formed in nonliterate, traditional cultures. Some authors (for example, Cole, 1990) claim that these prerequisites are present in all normally developing individuals and that it is only their expression that depends on specific symbolic means available in a given culture. Thus syllogistic reasoning, for example, is presumed to be already present in uneducated individuals; but they reveal this type of reasoning only in situations that are familiar and correspond to their cultural norm. There is, however, an opposing viewpoint that suggests that certain forms of reasoning appear only as a result of particular educational practices and cannot emerge spontaneously. According to this point of view, what appears as syllogistic reasoning in an uneducated individual is actually a result of everyday experience which, under specific problem-solving conditions, leads to the right answer. These two alternatives were tested by Tulviste (1979), an Estonian student of Luria. He studied syllogistic reasoning in children who belonged to a small nationality in eastern Siberia. These children attended school, but otherwise lived the life of traditional, preindustrial society. An important result of Tulviste's study showed that native children have greater success with syllogistic tasks involving hypothetical situations based on scientific material (unknown to the children) than with tasks based on familiar, everyday life events. This result indicates that syllogistic reasoning originates in systematic school-based learning activities, rather than in everyday experience.

Condition C is characteristic of individuals who have been exposed to higher-order psychological tools but have received no proper mediation of them. A prototypical case here would involve an individual whose everyday life is attuned to the norms of preliterate traditional society, but who at the same time has received formal schooling. Sometimes symbolic tools acquired at school remain unmediated, that is, they are used as tools in a narrow sense but fail to affect the whole of an individual's cognition. This phenomenon has been observed in immigrants from a third world country. They had more than twelve years of schooling, but still experienced great difficulties in solving problems intended for Israeli adolescents. These same immigrants demonstrated remarkably high learning potential, and improved their performance dramatically after being taught the Instrumental Enrichment program (Rosemarine et al., 1993). One may conclude that this group received adequate MLE in a traditional way, but was deprived of the proper mediation of symbolic tools.

A somewhat similar situation can be observed in children making the transition from one literate culture to another. Although these children have received adequate MLE in their original culture, the transition process disrupts mediated interaction, and the new set of psychological tools associated with their acquired culture remains poorly mediated. Severe learning problems have been observed in children from highly educated families because parents were unable or unwilling to mediate a new culture to their children (Kozulin and Venger, 1993).

Condition D is characteristic of individuals who have had no exposure to higher-order psychological tools, and whose traditional MLE acquisition has been disrupted. A prototypical case is a group of individuals who become displaced and whose traditional cultural transmission is disrupted by war, famine, or other major social upheaval. Often, this is a group whose members choose or were forced to abandon their traditional way of life and have found themselves on the margins of industrial society. The new position makes it impossible to continue traditional mediational practices, while higher-order psychological tools associated with school-based learning remain unavailable and unmediated (Feuerstein, 1991).

One should remember that the above matrix is in no way exhaustive and is not intended for simplistic classification. Each of the conditions outlined is a dynamic entity that can be transformed if proper educational and mediational efforts are made. In addition to his or her position in the matrix, a given individual may have problems with specific cognitive functions dependent on a given subculture. For example, an adequate, general MLE may coexist with a lack of mediation of the need for precision, because precision is not highly valued in a given subculture. This specific "deficiency" may cause certain problems of adaptation to a culture that values this trait highly. The ultimate criterion is that of modifiability. Individuals who exhibit high modifiability will be capable of changing their functioning in accordance with a new hierarchy of cultural demands.

# 4

## Cognitive Education

According to Vygotsky, the child's process of cognitive development and the process of instruction are interdependent. Certain educational practices, such as learning to write, require a new set of psychological functions. But once these functions emerge, they make the further development of systematic learning possible. Such an approach calls for a radical revision of the nomenclature of psychological processes. From the sociocultural point of view, such functions as attention, memory, or problem solving undergo a radical transformation once they become involved in the activities mediated by symbolic psychological tools. At the same time, instructionally based verbal functions such as reading and composition become new psychological processes that not only enhance the cognitive repertoire of the learner but can also serve as mediators for other cognitive processes. Cognitive development, therefore, cannot be seen in isolation from the instructional process that provides new forms of symbolic activity, eventually internalized as new cognitive formations.

In traditionally organized instruction there is no precise correspondence between the curve of cognitive development and the curve of instruction.

> Instruction has its own sequences and organization, it follows curriculum and a timetable, and its rules cannot be expected to coincide with the inner laws of the developmental process it calls to life . . . For example, the different steps in learning arithmetic may be of unequal value for mental development. It often happens that three of four steps in instruction add little to

the child's understanding of arithmetic, and then, with the fifth step, something clicks; the child has grasped a general principle, and his/her developmental curve rises markedly . . . When the child learns some operation of arithmetic or some scientific concept, the development of that operation or concept has only begun; the curve of development does not coincide with the curve of school instruction; by and large, instruction precedes development. (Vygotsky, 1986, p. 185)

Instruction, therefore, can be deliberately structured in such a way that apart from its role as a provider of information and concrete skills, it also promotes cognitive development. These early ideas of Vygotsky found their practical realization in the reorientation of the instructional process in the direction of cognitive education (Costa, 1985; Presseisen, 1987; Fischer, 1990; Swartz and Perkins, 1990). Cognitive education approaches can be loosely divided into three groups: content-based programs, infusion programs, and supplementary cognitive intervention programs. Vygotskian ideas have had their most obvious influence on content-based programs, where the task of cognitive development is intertwined with the task of developing students' conceptual reasoning in a given disciplinary field. At the same time, the notion of psychological tools has considerable potential for the development of supplementary cognitive intervention programs aimed at creating conditions for the appropriation of symbolic tools by those students who are lacking them. For this reason this chapter will emphasize the relevance of the psychological tools paradigm for "content-free" cognitive intervention.

## Content-Based Cognitive Education

Content-based programs presuppose that teaching thinking should be firmly embedded in the content material. In its most consistent form, content-based cognitive education was realized by Davydov (1988a) and other neo-Vygotskians in the Soviet Union and Eastern Europe (Lompscher, 1984; Karpov and Bransford, 1995). These neo-Vygotskians argued that in a properly designed and implemented curriculum, the development of thinking should be the inherent and, therefore, internal element. This thesis is based on the assumption of the theoretical nature of formal learning (see Chapter 3). Because the task of language, math, or history instruction is to create in the child a system of linguistic, mathematical, or historical concepts, the psychological problem of reasoning and concept formation should be incorporated into this overall educational task. The task of theoretical learning is to create in the child the generalized thinking models within the given field of knowledge, and thus such learning cannot fail to promote more generalized changes in the child's reasoning. From the sociocultural point of view mathematical or linguistic reasoning represents a form of historically developing human cognition and as such will help further the child's cognitive development. For example, it has been argued that the theoretical learning of the concept of number in primary school not only facilitates the child's mastery of such notions as negative numbers, decimal fractions, and elements of algebra, but also positively influences the child's ability to solve Piagetian conservation problems (see Karpov and Bransford, 1995).

Another attempt at constructing a content-based cognitive education program was undertaken by Lipman in his "Philosophy for Children" project (Lipman, Sharp, and Oscanyan, 1980). The original impulse behind this project was to satisfy the child's need for meaning. Acquisition of meaning in different areas is possible only through the development of thinking skills: "The integration of thinking skills into every aspect of the curriculum would sharpen children's capacity to make connections and draw distinctions, to define and to classify, to assess factual information objectively and critically, to deal reflectively with the relationship between facts and values, and to differentiate their beliefs and what is true from their understanding of what is logically possible" (Lipman, Sharp, and Oscanyan, 1980, p. 15).

Lipman argued that because philosophy preoccupied itself with the problem of precise, systematic, and reflective reasoning, it offered the best material for teaching thinking. The major problem here is to present philosophical reasoning tasks in a form suited to children. To resolve this problem Lipman created a number of short novels that included material suitable for classroom discussion that would lead to the development of philosophical reasoning skills. Teachers participating in the project are instructed how to play the role of the facilitator who creates the conditions of a genuine dialogue. Lipman's program can be considered content-based because it is grounded in specific content material (a "philosophical novel"). Its originality is in constructing this material rather then taking it ready-made from classical sources such as Plato's dialogues or Descartes's *Method*. Evaluation of the "Philosophy for Children" program (Lipman 1985; Bransford et al., 1985) indicates that the program indeed leads to cognitive and learning-skills enhancement in both inner-city and suburban children.

## Cognitive Infusion Programs

The most popular form of cognitive education programs are, however, the so-called infusion programs (Swartz and Perkins, 1990). The rationale of such programs is to infuse teaching about thinking into the regular school curriculum. One of the popular methodologies of the infusion is a critical thinking approach (Halpern, 1989; Fischer, 1990). Children can be taught how to question statements or texts offered to them in school. For example, instead of simply asking children to read and retell the story of Goldilocks and the Three Bears the teacher may teach them to ask and answer the following questions:

> "What happened in the story?"
> "Why did Goldilocks like Little Bear's bed best?"
> "What would you have done if you were Goldilocks?"
> "Can you think of a different ending?"

If successful, the reading lesson will then become an occasion for the development in children of such cognitive skills as analysis, attribution, hypothetical reasoning, and so on.

The same approach can also be used in math. Instead of asking children to solve a standard arithmetic problem (for example, "There are 60 children and each of them has 2 hot dogs. How many hot dogs will the children eat?"), the teacher may offer them an opportunity to create a problem of their own. For example, students may be asked to create a problem that will involve children and hot dogs and will have an answer of 120 hot dogs. While in a standard task students can disregard the levels of analysis and problem formulation and go directly to the selection of the proper operation (multiplication), in the cognitively oriented task they will have to analyze the available data, to create a plan, to formulate the question, to check the question against the given answer, and so on. The analysis of problems created by different students may contribute both to a better understanding of the process of problem solving and to a realization of the divergent nature of thinking (for example, that the same answer can correspond to a number of tasks).

Different authors suggest infusing different types of reasoning operations into the regular curriculum. For example, Fischer (1990) suggested that sequencing, classifying, judging, predicting, advancing hypotheses, self-reflection, and taking the other's point of view are the most important elements of critical thinking. But while discussing how to teach students such an important cognitive skill as a transfer of learning, Fogarthy, Perkins, and Barell (1992) mention using analogies, generalizing concepts, anticipating applications, doing parallel problem solving, and performing metacognitive reflection. Such a diversity of candidates for cognitive infusion constitutes both the major attraction and the major problem for infusion programs. On the one hand, freedom in selecting the cognitive principles that are most appropriate for a given student population and a given segment of the curriculum is quite attractive. Using one of many available cognitive infusion programs, teachers can create their own cognitive education lesson or program (see, for example, Beyer, 1991). On the other hand, the effectiveness of these programs depends almost exclusively on the teacher's ability to assess the students' cognitive needs, find a proper balance between the curricular content and the cognitive principles, and apply the selected principles systematically. Most infusion programs are eclectic, that is, they are not based on any particular cognitive or learning theory and are used in an ad hoc manner. Because of this, infusion programs often remain poorly coordinated with the conceptual structure of the curricular material.

## Psychological Tools as a Basis for Cognitive Intervention

Psychological tools are those symbolic artifacts—signs, symbols, texts, formulae, graphic-symbolic devices—with the help of which individuals master their own "natural" psychological functions of perception, memory, attention, and so on. The involvement of psychological tools engenders new psychological functions that are sociocultural in their origin and superindividual in their nature. The acquisition of higher-order psychological tools constitutes the necessary prerequisite for successful formal schooling. Hypothetical reasoning, theoretical experimenting, the use of models, generalized problem solving, and other scholastic activities cannot be accomplished without some form of symbolic representation based on the use of psychological tools.

The acquisition, internalization, and use of psychological tools are essential elements of this cognitive aspect of instruction. In regular educational practice the role of psychological tools is often obscured by the fact that the acquisition of content material and psychological tools is intertwined. Under certain conditions, however, the normative acquisition of psychological tools is impeded. This happens when these tools have been unavailable in the child's native culture (for example, a preliterate traditional society), or when an individual's specific handicap (for example, blindness) interferes with the appropriation of psychological tools available to others. The acquisition and use of psychological tools can therefore be studied in two contexts: (1) in the context of regular development and formal education that includes acquisition of psychological tools as an integral element of the learning process; and (2) in the context of special cognitive intervention programs that provide psychological tools to students who for one reason or another are lacking them.

## The Appropriation of Psychological Tools and the Mediated Learning Experience

The process of the appropriation of psychological tools differs from the process of content learning. This difference reflects the fact that while content learning material often reproduces empirical realities familiar to students in their everyday lives, psychological tools are cultural artifacts that are acquired in the course of special learning activities. For example, a content knowledge item such as the fact that Boston is the capital of Massachusetts corresponds to empirical reality and can be known or learned by students both spontaneously or as a part of the school curriculum. Contrarily, a tool such as a geographical map and its legend can be acquired only in the course of a special learning activity. A map's legend is a conventional artifact that helps students to find any geographical entity—for example, a capital of certain country, even when both the country in question and its capital are unknown to the student. For this reason the acquisition of psychological tools requires a learning paradigm different from the acquisition of content knowledge. The required learning paradigm presupposes:

a. A learning process that is deliberate rather than spontaneous;
b. The systemic acquisition of tools, because they are systemically organized; and
c. An emphasis on the generalized nature of tools and their use.

In comparing these requirements with the universal criteria of Mediated Learning Experience (MLE)—intentionality, transcendence, and mediation of meaning (Feuerstein, 1990; see also Chapter 3)—one can perceive a considerable overlap between them. This overlap is not surprising, because the role of MLE is to create cognitive prerequisites essential for successful direct learning. Many of these cognitive prerequisites are closely related to the use of symbolic tools. It is useful, then, to explore the relationship between the criteria of MLE interaction and conditions of psychological tools acquisition.

## Intentionality

As mentioned above, the acquisition of psychological tools must have the character of a deliberate action. If there is no intentionality on the part of the teacher-mediator, psychological tools will not be appropriated, or will be acquired as another content item, rather than as a tool. Sometimes teachers fail to focus students' attention on symbolic tools that are presented with content-learning material. As a result students receive tools together with content in a syncretic, undifferentiated manner, and are unable to identify the instrumental part of the learning material.

## Transcendence

By their very nature, psychological tools are generalized. A tool fulfills its role only if it is appropriated as a generalized instrument capable of organizing individual cognitive and learning processes in different contexts and in application to different tasks. That is why the failure to teach psychological tools in a transcendent manner inevitably leads to the failure of their appropriation by the students. Apparently this is exactly what happens when school-based instruction in reading, writing, and mathematics is carried out purely as content and skills training without the mediation of the generalized instrumental function of these symbolic tool systems. As a result literacy and mathematical skills remain isolated and fail to influence the overall cognitive and problem-solving abilities of students (Kozulin and Lurie, 1994).

## Mediation of Meaning

Mediation of meaning is an essential moment in the acquisition of psychological tools, because symbolic tools derive their meaning only from the cultural conventions that engendered them. In a sense symbolic tools (for example, letters, codes, mathematical signs) have no meaning whatsoever outside the cultural convention that infuses them with meaning and purpose. If this purpose is poorly mediated to learners, a proper understanding of the tools' instrumental function will not be achieved. For example, a foreign language is sometimes taught as a coding system that simply maps the correspondence between foreign words and words in the native language of the learner. As a result the learner becomes severely handicapped in both comprehension of and expression in the foreign language. If on the contrary the purpose of foreign language study is mediated as an ability to comprehend and formulate meaningful propositions, students become capable of grasping the instrumental role of a foreign sign system.

Apart from pointing to the necessary condition for the successful appropriation of psychological tools, MLE theory has also served as a foundation for an extremely elaborate system of cognitive intervention—the Instrumental Enrichment program (Feuerstein et al., 1980), which among other goals provides psychological tools to learners who are lacking them.

## Instrumental Enrichment Viewed as a Synthesis of Psychological Tools and MLE

Usually the Instrumental Enrichment (IE) program is discussed as one of the supplementary cognitive intervention programs aimed at developing thinking skills in their "pure" form (Bransford et al., 1985; Fischer,

1990). The difference between these supplementary programs and the infusion programs lies in their relationship to content material and in the organization of the program itself. Infusion programs take educational content material as a basis and infuse certain cognitive skills into the students' work with this material. As a result the content material is mastered with a greater awareness of the student's own cognitive operations. In the supplementary cognitive intervention programs, cognitive skills become the central target of intervention. Special lessons are allocated to teaching thinking skills. The program itself is composed of special exercises that are relatively content free, in the sense that they are not linked to any specific disciplinary knowledge or school skills. The advantage of such an approach is its ability to foster in students generalized thinking patterns that are content free and that can then be applied to a great variety of contents.

IE (Feuerstein et al., 1980) was first conceived of as a method for developing learning potential in socioculturally disadvantaged adolescents, many of them belonging to minority ethnic groups. It was argued that both the low level of scholastic achievement and the low level of general cognitive performance of these students were products of the insufficient development or inefficient use of the cognitive functions that serve as prerequisites of effective thinking and learning. The source of these cognitive deficiencies was seen in the inadequate amount or type of mediated learning experience of the students. IE was thus designed as a remedial and enrichment program that would provide students with a mediated learning experience, correct their deficient cognitive functions, teach them the necessary basic concepts, vocabulary, and operations, foster reflective reasoning, and turn them from passive recipients of information into active learners.

MLE theory, as noted, served as an explicit theoretical foundation for the development of the IE program. The concept of psychological tools and Vygotsky's sociocultural theory were absent in the original theoretical design of this program. It seems, however, that what IE material can offer is a fruitful synthesis of psychological tools and MLE paradigms. Moreover, the analysis of IE from the perspective of psychological tools may produce a set of principles suitable for the design of new cognitive intervention programs utilizing the MLE and psychological tools approach.

The IE program uses materials that are content free. Activities with these materials are process oriented, and each IE instrument and the IE battery as a whole are systemically organized. The content-free nature of IE materials helps students to master them as tools directed primarily at their own cognitive processes. IE materials incorporate a large number of graphic-symbolic devices such as schematic representations, tables, charts, graphs. All these devices constitute psychological tools that facilitate the student's transition from direct interaction with material to an interaction mediated by symbolic devices. Activities in the IE program include coding and decoding, the use of models and formulae, representation of one and the same problem in different modalities, generalization, and classification. All these activities in their essence are directed at the appropriation and internalization of psychological tools and ultimately at the development of higher psychological functions dependent on these tools. The emphasis on process rather than product leads to the development of metacognitive awareness and control, which are the constituent features of higher psychological functions. One of the central characteristics of higher psychological functions based on psychological tools is their systemic nature, which the IE program actively promotes. IE instruments are designed in a way that induces the repeated integration of cognitive functions developed with the help of tasks located in different places within one instrument and within different instruments. The same cognitive principles reappear in different instruments in various modalities. One of the central goals of IE as a cognitive intervention program is to make symbolic psychological tools available to students who, because of their cultural difference, educational deprivation, or other circumstances, have been deprived of these tools. IE provides an "artificial" system of cognitive development, which under more favorable conditions unfolds in a "natural" way.

## *Psychological Tools within the IE Program*

As an example, let us consider psychological tools as they can be identified within one of the "Categorization" exercises of the IE program (see Figure 4.1).

    *CODES* Coding, or the substitution of a simple sign (for example, a letter or digit) for an object or concept, constitutes one of the most

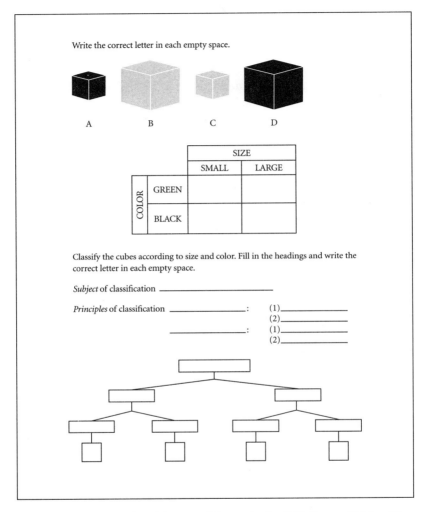

Figure 4.1 Instrumental Enrichment—"Categorization." (Arlington Heights, Ill.: IRI/SkyLight, 1996, © R. Feuerstein, HWCRI.)

basic operations associated with symbolic tools. Through coding individuals become freed from the immediacy of objects with which they are operating or about which they are thinking. The first step in this direction is naming, the substitution of a word for a thing. Coding, when an even more arbitrary selected sign is used as a temporary substitute for an object or a word, represents the next step. Unlike words that are "attached" to their objects, codes are detached from them. Depending on circumstances the same code, such as A, B, C, or I, II, III, can serve as a substitute for entirely different objects or processes. On one of the workbook pages A, B, C can denote different cubes; on the next page the same code can denote different pencils or cities. Coding brings to the learners' experience the quality of radical distancing between the plane of objects and the plane of mental operations with them. Students' facility with algebraic expressions, geometric notations, physical formulae, and geographical legends is built on the foundation of coding. Coding provides specific means of communication that are generalized enough so that the personal experiences of interlocutors do not interfere with the essential messages. When somebody writes about "right angle B, of the isosceles triangle ABC," the coding of angles provides enough information for a reader to comprehend this triangle without actually seeing it. Coding also provides one of the most transparent instances of representation. In the context of the exercises in Figure 4.1 the letter A represents the small black cube with all its properties and features. The student learns how to manipulate the representation of the cube without actually dragging the cube along. Thus the codes of different cubes can be entered into the matrix and into the tree diagram. Instead of working with objects, students learn how to rely on coded representations.

The same page allows us to return to the issue of coding when digits (1) (2), (1) (2) suggest different classification opportunities, for example, Color: (1) green, (2) black; or Size: (1) large, (2) small. Here the principle of coding marks the number of different opportunities. Coding thus becomes numbering or enumeration.

*MATRICES* The matrix is one of the graphic-symbolic devices widely used in contemporary learning materials. The goal of graphic-symbolic devices is to provide the organizational format for the data with which students are working. If the regular flow of a textbook or lecture narrative provides the syntagmatic organization of data, graphic-symbolic devices, like the matrix, offer a paradigmatic organization. It is with the help of graphic-symbolic devices that an item (for example, a word, object, concept, number) becomes defined within a system. For example, the large black cube in Figure 4.1, when placed in the matrix, becomes an item occupying a proper cell within the total system defined by the parameters of color and size.

The use of matrices also gives the student an opportunity to contemplate different possibilities and compare them with actualities. Let us imagine that only three cubes (A, B, C) are presented in Figure 4.1. If no graphic-symbolic device is offered, the student may stop at just comparing the available objects. Working with a matrix, the student can realize that within it there is an additional possibility for a cube that is black and large. Providing a systemic framework matrix thus not only helps the student to organize data but also to see possibilities that are not yet actualized. Once internalized, the matrix becomes a powerful psychological tool for analyzing objects into constituent parameters, grouping these parameters and projecting new combinations that may eventually lead to the construction of the new items.

For example, the matrix in Table 4.1 may help the student to organize different events belonging to the real as well as the imaginary past, present, and future. In this way historical, literary, and personal experience can be properly discussed and analyzed.

Learning the principle of matrices also prepares students for standard psychometric tasks. In these tasks the parameters of the matrix are "hidden" and should be discovered through the analysis of items within the matrix. The matrix in Figure 4.2 gives some idea of the principles on which such tasks are constructed. The students should first explore the field of data and realize that the parameters in this task include three elements, a, b, and c, arranged in certain sequences. To identify the nature of these sequences the students should analyze rows and columns of the matrix. Analysis of the top row helps to form the hypothesis regarding the rule of change in rows ($n$, $n + 1$, $n + 2$); analysis of the columns suggests that elements all appear in the middle and bottom rows in the same quantities as in the top row. Combination of the first and second rule helps to predict the missing element: the first rule will predict 5 "c" elements; the second rule will predict 3 "a" elements.

*Table 4.1*   **Matrix of events**

|                   | Past | Present | Future |
| ----------------- | ---- | ------- | ------ |
| Real events       |      |         |        |
| Imaginary events  |      |         |        |

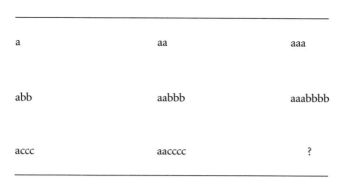

|       |        |          |
|-------|--------|----------|
| a     | aa     | aaa      |
| abb   | aabbb  | aaabbbb  |
| accc  | aacccc | ?        |

Figure 4.2  Matrix task.

For students unfamiliar with thinking in terms of a matrix the problem in Figure 4.2 may pose a serious problem, because it provides no explicit framework for the analysis of data. By applying the cognitive tool of the matrix, the same data that only recently seemed to be chaotic appears systematically arranged according to certain rules.

*TREE DIAGRAMS* In the task in Figure 4.1 the role of the tree diagram is to provide a graphic-symbolic tool that helps to capture the process of classification. Unlike the matrix and the table, which lack the dynamic aspect of data organization, the tree diagram allows one to trace the consecutive steps of the classification process. For example, one may start by dividing all cubes into black and green, and only at the second level of classification divide each of these groups into large and small. Another student may select an alternate strategy, starting with division according to size, followed by division according to color. In both cases the tree diagram will help to register the selected sequence of classification steps.

A more general goal of the tree diagram as a symbolic tool is to embody the evolutionary principle of continuity and differentiation. Tree diagrams have featured prominently in the creation of representations corresponding to the genetic-evolutionary approach to the origin and evolution of species. Tree diagrams capture both the continuity of biological evolution and the differentiation of species. A somewhat similar tree diagram is used for the depiction of the language families. Through the use of these diagrams a historical-evolutionary approach to the development, differentiation, and relationships among languages is implanted in the learner's mind. Once the tree diagram is internalized as a psychological tool, it can help the student to think about familiar phenomena in a new and creative way. For example, the growth and differentiation of several towns that ultimately form a metropolitan area (for example, greater Boston) can be presented as a tree diagram, thus leading students to a better and more process-oriented comprehension of urban development.

## The Systemic Character of the Program

In the cognitive intervention program designed according to the psychological tools paradigm, all elements should be systemically integrated. In this respect the very content of different units of the IE program calls for systemic activities. In the "Analytic Perception" unit the task is to analyze the whole into constituent parts and to integrate the parts into the whole. In the "Comparisons," "Categorization," and "Syllogisms" units all tasks presuppose identification of the elements as parts of the system. "Family Relations" explores a system of relationships based on family trees. "Orientation in Space" calls for the identification of an object's position in different orientation systems, and so on.

In addition to the content, the organization of IE materials and IE-based learning activities leads to systemic orientation. IE materials are designed and organized in such a way that each individual task is related to the whole system of tasks in a given unit. For example, all tasks of the "Organization of Dots" unit have the same nature—looking at a cloud of dots, a student is required to discern figures shown in the model and then reproduce these figures by connecting the proper dots. At the same time, each page has a different model and each specific task has a different constellation of dots. As a result each task within this instrument appears as a unique version of the general task paradigm. Successful work with these tasks depends on the student's ability to develop a number of general problem-solving strategies. Thus the solution of each individual task requires access to general strategies and comparisons with previous tasks. In this way work with each individual task becomes an element in the total IE system.

It should be noted that successful solving of particular problems does not constitute the ultimate goal of IE. It is much more important for the student to discover the general cognitive principles underlying the IE tasks, to formulate these principles, and to be able to extend or "bridge" them to other areas of learning. The need to establish a cognitive principle requires the student to take a systemic approach to the material; one cannot establish such a principle if the task is perceived as an isolated element unconnected to other tasks. This systemic orientation is further augmented by the procedure of "bridging" the cognitive principle to the other domains. Let us take the principle that a task can have one, several, or unlimited number of correct solutions. This principle can be discovered and formulated in the course of work with IE's "Orientation in Space I" unit. Once this principle is "bridged" to such areas as mathematics, language arts, and everyday experience, these areas cease to be isolated domains within the learner's mind and become systemically connected through the unifying cognitive principle.

The issue of "bridging" has already taken us beyond the systemic role of IE materials and into the field of IE-based activities. These activities include repeated comparisons between newer and older tasks. One of the standard elements of IE teaching is the question: "Tell me, how does this task (page) differ from the previous one?" Another typical activity is the recollection of earlier instances when a certain cognitive principle, operation, or function has appeared. For example: "Yes, the first task has only one, while the second has an unlimited number of correct solutions. Tell me, in which of the previous units have we discovered the same situation?"

The systemic orientation of the IE program closely resembles Vygotskian requirements for the systemic organization of "scientific" concepts. Vygotsky (1986) distinguishes between spontaneous empirical concepts that are mostly unsystematic and that reflect the everyday experience of the child, and "scientific" or academic concepts that are formed in the framework of formal schooling and that are systemically organized: "Scientific concepts would be unnecessary if they were reflecting mere appearances of objects, as empirical concepts do. The scientific concept thus stands in a different relation to the object, in a relation achievable only in conceptual form, which, in its turn, is possible only through a system of concepts. From this point of view, any real concept must be taken only together with its system of relations that determines its measure of generality. A concept is like a living cell that must be viewed only together with its offshoots penetrating into surrounding tissues" (Vygotsky, 1986, p. 173).

## Progressive Organization of the Program

The IE program has a progressive organization, so that cognitive functions, operations, and skills developed with the help of units that are taught in the beginning of the program help students to master more complex tasks when they reach more advanced units. For example, "Organization of Dots" is usually taught at the very beginning of the IE program. One of the important concepts introduced in this unit is the concept of the *model*, which is used in virtually all subsequent instruments. The notion of *comparison*, in contrast, is presented within this instrument in a rather circumscribed way, as a comparison between different geometric figures. The same notion of comparison becomes a major learning target later on in the unit "Comparisons." Within this unit comparisons are made in different domains (for example, pictorial, graphical-schematic, and verbal), on different levels of abstraction, and with the help of different operations. Later on this thorough exploration of the comparative function becomes a foundation for approaching the tasks in more advanced units such as "Categorizations" and "Syllogisms." These advanced units are poorly understood by students without preparation in the field of comparisons. Thus the progressive organization of the IE program is based on first introducing basic elements that later reappear as parts of more complex structures or functions.

## Cognitive Principles throughout the Program

Unlike many other cognitive education programs, IE focuses predominantly on general cognitive principles and strategies rather than on specific operations. This is why the same cognitive principle reappears within the IE program many times, each time in a new context and with the help of a different modality of presentation. Let us consider the following principle: "A task may have one, several, or an unlimited number of correct solutions." This principle is first introduced in a systematic way in the "Orientation in Space I" unit in conjunction with the presentation of similar-looking tasks, of which some have one and some an unlimited number of correct solutions (Figure 4.3). The same cognitive principle reappears in "Comparisons" (Figure 4.4). Here again

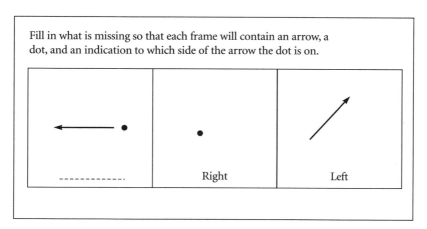

Figure 4.3 Instrumental Enrichment—"Orientation in Space." (Arlington Heights, Ill.: IRI/SkyLight, 1996, © R. Feuerstein, HWCRI.)

the superficial similarity of the appearance of the tasks should not deceive the students. In some of the tasks there is only one correct solution, which should be identified by circling the correct parameters; in other tasks there are multiple correct solutions, each of them dependent on specific figures drawn by the student. The same principle reappears in the more difficult units of the IE program.

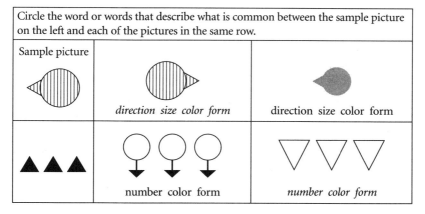

Figure 4.4 Instrumental Enrichment—"Comparisons."(Arlington Heights, Ill.: IRI/SkyLight, 1996, © R. Feuerstein, HWCRI.)

## Higher-Order Psychological Tools—Form as Content, Content as Form

As research and evaluation of the IE program demonstrate (Ben-Hur, 1994; Savell, Twohig, and Rachford, 1986), supplementary cognitive intervention programs can be quite effective in enhancing the learning potential and cognitive performance of disadvantaged students. A more complex question involves the relationships between cognitive intervention and content learning. From the perspective of the psychological tools paradigm, the problem of the relationships between "form" (cognitive) and "content" (disciplinary) calls for the analysis of those higher-order symbolic systems that are intimately related to specific fields of study. The higher-order psychological tools, acting in sophisticated learning contexts, enter into new and more complex relationships with the content material. Let us explore these relationships in two contexts, that of physics and literary studies.

The unique difficulty in learning physics stems from the fact that a student's everyday empirical knowledge of physical phenomena does not correspond to the content material of physical science. For this reason teaching physics involves a number of steps. First, basic physical concepts (for example, force and mass) are presented to the learner; next, material created with the help of these concepts is related to the observable reality of physical phenomena; then the conceptual material is "translated" into symbolic form with the help of mathematical tools; and finally the formalized conceptual system can be used for prediction of empirical phenomena.

What distinguishes the use of symbolic tools in physics is their dependence on physical concepts. While basic psychological tools can be used universally in different fields of study, the higher-order psychological tools become dependent on the specific field. In order to use "F" as a sign for "force" in physical formulae, a student must acquire psychological tools on two different levels. On a basic level the student should be familiar with the operation of coding an object or process according to cultural convention. On a higher level, however, the student should acquire the function of the symbolic representation of concepts, because "force" is not an object or an event, but a concept. Thus on the higher levels of learning psychological tools become conceptual tools. Such a transformation poses an important question regarding the scope and limits of content-free cognitive education based on the idea of psychological tools. As long as the subject of such education is basic-level psychological tools, the outcome of such education is the development of cognitive strategies applicable in all possible contexts. But when the appropriation of psychological tools becomes dependent on the formation of a specific (for example, physical) concept, one can hardly speak about content-free cognitive education. The cognitive aspect becomes incorporated into the conceptual structure of learning physics.

A somewhat similar situation can be observed in the field of literary study. Once full literacy is acquired by the learner, the instrumental aspect of text comprehension becomes obscured by the content analysis of literary works read by the student. The focus of learning is on the events, ideas, and characters of the literary work. At the same time there are reasons to believe that a literary work can serve as a supertool, supplying its readers with new instruments for the comprehension of life events (Kozulin, 1993; see also Chapter 6). It is important to remember, however, that this instrumental function of the literary work is based on its formal elements rather than on its "content." From this perspective one may consider Jorge Luis Borges's stories primarily as psychological tools that enable his readers to project new relationships between text and reality. In Borges's stories life is secondary to a text and reproduces the constraints and regulations of the text production. By acquiring this schema as a tool, Borges's readers may open new perspectives in their perception of social and historical events. As in the study of physics, the question arises whether there is a domain specificity in the acquisition of such higher-order psychological tools. It seems probable that only through the special mediation of literary texts can their instrumental qualities become appropriated by readers.

The concept of psychological tools can, therefore, be used on different levels in cognitive education. On a more basic level, the acquisition of psychological tools is indispensable for the generalized forms of data analysis, comparison, planning, and problem solving. On higher levels, more sophisticated psychological tools function as a part of the conceptual apparatus of a given disciplinary field both in the sciences and in the humanities.

# 5 ✥

# Cognitive Skills in Immigrant and Ethnic Minority Students

The problem of immigrant and ethnic minority students' cognitive and problem-solving skills has both theoretical and practical significance. As a theoretical problem it raises the question of cross-cultural differences in cognition and their influence on education. As a practical problem it emerges each time a teacher enters a culturally heterogeneous classroom with the aim of providing students with the skills necessary for a successful formal education.

## Cross-Cultural Differences in Cognition

There are several approaches to the problem of cross-cultural differences in cognition. Some are based on a belief in the basic uniformity of human cognition, with differences explained as quantitative in nature; others emphasize the formative influence of culture, leading to the heterogeneity of cognitive performances and styles.

First, let us consider what may be called a *psychometric* model of ethnic differences in cognition. This model originates in the nineteenth-century idea of the evolutionary development of cognition in different ethnic groups (Tylor, 1871). Within this model human cognition is perceived as basically uniform, although its development and progress have occurred unevenly in different ethnic groups. Culture as such does not play an important role, being perceived as an aggregate of individual cognitive efforts.

The most recent revival of this model, cast in psychometric terms, was undertaken by Richard Herrnstein and Charles Murray (1994) in *The Bell Curve*. Herrnstein and Murray took for granted the basic uniformity of human cognition and the feasibility of assessing it with the help of standard psychometric IQ tests. They then demonstrate differences in the IQ scores of different ethnic groups. They conclude that cognitive skills are unevenly distributed, with some ethnic groups being more proficient (East Asians) and others less (African Americans). Herrnstein and Murray believe that intellectual abilities have a strong genetic component, and they are rather pessimistic concerning the role of learning in the development of cognitive skills.

For the purposes of the present discussion, it is important to emphasize that the major weakness of the psychometric approach lies in its reluctance to discuss the nature of cognitive processes (Feuerstein and Kozulin, 1995). The complexity of human intelligence is extreme, thus calling for the expansion of our research approaches rather than their reduction. Unfortunately, Herrnstein and Murray chose an extremely reductionist position in equating the assessment of intelligence with IQ measurement. Throughout the book the authors rely on data from a longitudinal study using four subtests of the Armed Forces Qualification Test as a measure of IQ (Herrnstein and Murray, 1994, app. 3). The four chosen subtests were Word Knowledge, Paragraph Comprehension, Arithmetic Reasoning, and Mathematical Knowledge. There is little doubt that one can measure the number of words recognized or mathematical operations accurately performed. The question is whether such a measurement can be presented as an assessment of intelligence. How is it possible to claim that IQ measured in this way is unaffected by education? The authors' far-reaching conclusions are based on the following chain of reductions: first, intelligence is equated with the results of test performance, then the whole range of possible tests is reduced to a few knowledge-based tasks performed within a limited time frame, after which the data obtained are interpreted far beyond their actual empirical base.

An opposite, culture-centered approach to cognitive skills was proposed in 1930 by Vygotsky and Luria (1993) and developed by their followers (Tulviste, 1991). This approach places a major emphasis on culture as a source of differences in cognition. According to Vygotsky and his followers, cognitive processes are formed in the course of sociocultural activities. As a result, the individual comes into possession of a variety of cognitive processes engendered by different activities and requested by different types of activity. The radical change in cognition is associated in this model with the transition from one set of symbolic psychological tools to another. Psychological tools, as we have seen, include signs, symbolic and literacy systems, graphic-symbolic devices, and formulae. Intercultural cognitive differences are attributed to the variance in systems of psychological tools and in the methods of their acquisition practiced in other cultures. According to Vygotskians formal learning places specific cognitive demands on students, requiring facility with decontextualized symbolic systems of representation, hypothetical modeling, and reflection. Minority students whose native culture does not have the required set of psychological tools should be introduced to them in order to acquire the necessary cognitive skills.

Critical examination of the Vygotskian approach has led Cole (1990; Cole et al., 1971) to the "contextual" theory of cognitive functions. In a number of studies he and his colleagues examined the relationship between formal schooling and cognitive processes and came to the conclusion that different cultural and educational groups use the same basic cognitive processes. The manifestation of these processes, however, differs significantly depending on the context. For example, it seems that individuals belonging to different cultural groups all possess the ability to classify objects and phenomena. Their success in specific classification tasks will differ, however, depending on the contexts of classification. Unschooled subjects will fail at classification tasks characteristic of school-learning contexts and succeed with classification relevant to their everyday practical experience. Therefore, for the minority student the problem lies not so much in the acquisition of cognitive skills, but rather in becoming accustomed to the specific tasks and activities required by formal schooling. Cole (1990) draws a significant conclusion, saying that the relevance of school-based skills will grow as outside-the-school contexts become more similar to those of the school itself.

Within the mediated learning paradigm (Feuerstein et al., 1980; Feuerstein, Klein, and Tannenbaum, 1991) discussed in Chapter 3, an important distinction is made between cognitive differences caused by cultural distance and those caused by the individual's deprivation within his or her own culture. This paradigm is based on the notion of mediated learning experience (MLE) as opposed to direct unmediated learning. It is postulated that each culture has its own MLE-based systems of transmission from generation to generation. Individuals who have received adequate MLE in their native culture are expected to develop sufficient learning potential for a relatively unproblematic transition to their new culture. Those who were deprived of MLE in their own culture, however, manifest a reduced learning potential that makes their transition to the new culture and educational system problematic. An integrated model based on the interaction between psychological tools and the MLE paradigms discussed in Chapter 3 suggests that the minority students' learning problems may stem both from their lack of mastery of higher-order psychological tools and from their lack of proper MLE in either their native or their new culture. A crucial misstep occurs when the system of psychological tools relevant to the new culture is introduced in a direct, unmediated way. As a result the cognitive skills and functions associated with these tools are acquired by the minority student in a partial, local way and remain detached from the whole of his or her cognitive structure.

## Education in Traditional Societies and Adaptation to Formal Schooling

The educational problems of immigrant children can often be directly linked to the absence or inadequacy of earlier experiences of formal learning. Learning in traditional societies occurs in frameworks radically different from those prevalent in industrial societies. Following are three examples of the integration of traditional learners into modern educational systems. The first example presents the case of adult Hmong immigrants in the United States, the second, problems experienced by black children in South African schools, and the third, the integration of new immigrants from Ethiopia into the Israeli educational system.

The Hmong people are an ethnic tribe that lives in the highlands of Southeast Asia. As a result of military conflicts in this region, several thousand Hmong became refugees in the United States. Although the Hmong have traditionally relied on subsistence agriculture, in the United States they were resettled in urban areas. The history of a written language among the Hmong is somewhat controversial, but for all practical purposes the majority of Hmong were unfamiliar with either literacy or educational institutions. Hmong children learned practical skills from their parents or village elders. There was a clear gender differentiation of learning, with girls prepared to perform household tasks and boys trained for leadership roles. Gender expectations seem to be deeply engraved into the minds of Hmong women, who were supposed to farm, cook, and sew while men met, told stories, planned for the future, and worked with ideas (Collingnon Filipek, 1994).

The problems confronting this type of refugee or immigrant can be seen in the experience of Hmong women attending English literacy (ESL) classes. The issue of gender roles has already been mentioned. Hmong women were horrified when placed in the same ESL class with men, because they could not conceive of a universal learning context suitable for men and women alike. Learning for these women was firmly connected with certain practical gender-differentiated activity. Decontextualized literacy-based learning had to be introduced to them as a special new form of activity.

A second problem stems from the fact that the dominant activity of Hmong women is sewing "paj ntaub" (Collingnon Filipek, 1994). "Paj ntaub," literally "cloth flower," is a textile art that includes reverse appliqué and cross-stitch and other stitches embroidered on solid-colored or batik-dyed cloth. The "paj ntaub" are used as pillow covers, hanging ornaments, and also for ritual purposes. "Paj ntaub" can be considered the central activity in the life of a Hmong woman. Every girl is supposed to learn to sew "paj ntaub," and her level of skill is one criterion for her selection for marriage.

Learning "paj ntaub" requires considerable attention to what the master sewer, usually the mother, does—the girl acquires the skill by imitation, copying, correcting mistakes, copying again, and so on. Collingnon Filipek observed that in the course of teaching ESL to Hmong women, it became clear that they preferred the same imitative type of learning corresponding to the apprenticeship model known to them: "In conversing about the transcript of her earlier interview, Ploua realized that she preferred teachers who employ the same process her mother used in teaching her: sew a stitch, wait for Ploua to copy, instruct her to change the stitch if it did not match, do another until it matches, and then encourage her to try alone" (Collingnon Filipek, 1994, p. 339).

Such an approach to learning fits poorly with contemporary educational methods that emphasize meaning-based comprehension, student-initiated communication, and problem solving. Teachers are often reluctant to use repetition and drill because they themselves find them boring. Apparently this is not so for Hmong learners. Collingnon Filipek (1994, p. 340) concludes: "Monotonous to me, repetition to her meant learning . . . Practices—such as dictation or copying—are not distasteful for people who have integrated them as a part of well-developed functional systems for learning." The question remains, however, whether repetition and imitation are sufficient means for preparing immigrant learners for decontextualized problem solving, spontaneous composition of written texts, and flexibility in transferring cognitive strategies from one subject domain to another—in other words, whether reliance on traditional styles of learning will prepare immigrant students for the challenges of modern society beyond the acquisition of basic literacy.

The Hmong refugees in the United States are an example of a relatively small minority group that has found itself immersed in modern industrial society. In postapartheid South Africa, members of the black majority, including millions of students, found themselves in conditions quite similar to those of an immigrant minority. If for the Hmong learners the problem was how to make the transition from informal practical-skills learning to formal literacy-based education, for the South Africans the problem has been how to change the inadequate system of school-based education.

> Firstly, although the pupils' mother tongue and home language is Zulu, English is used as the medium of instruction for all subjects beyond Standard 2 [fourth grade]. Therefore, any inadequacies in the teaching and learning of English compound the other difficulties experienced by pupils in the learning of school subjects. Many teachers have only a basic command of English and an equally basic understanding of their subject matter. Secondly, large class sizes and a wide range of pupil ability within any one class cause difficulties which most teachers attempt to solve by means of a rigid and didactic teaching style aimed at inducing rote learning of material. This is reinforced by the frequent and rigid system of "control tests" and examinations which require only recall of information given in the specific words used by the teacher. (Adams and Wallace, 1993, p. 46)

This rigid teaching style is unfortunately not a unique product of the apartheid system, and apparently remains predominant in other African countries as well. On the one hand, the curriculum does not reflect the traditional tasks of the students' everyday life (Serpell, 1993). On the other, classroom instruction does not provide students with complex and flexible problem-solving skills that would allow them to succeed in technology-based occupations (Omokhodion, 1989).

Finally, we consider educational practices among Jews in rural Ethiopia, prior to their emigration to Israel that began in the mid-1980s and continues to this day. Like any other ethnic/cultural group, Ethiopian Jews have their specific features (Kaplan and Rosen, 1995; Wagaw, 1993). This specificity notwithstanding, their educational practices seem to be quite similar to those of other African groups (cf. Serpell, 1993). The majority of Ethiopian children receive their learning experiences in the home setting. These experiences include the oral transmission of their religious traditions and stories from parent to child. In addition to this oral transmission, children receive training in manual skills and craftsmanship. These skills are acquired in apprenticeship-like situations where the children learn by imitation and by focusing on the work habits of their parents or elder siblings. In addition to hearing many stories that they are encouraged to memorize, children often observe adults entertaining one another by creating spontaneous verses in Amharic. In this way children learn to appreciate the subtleties of language and to value the ability to produce and memorize poems, riddles, and proverbs (Rosen, 1989).

A more structured learning environment is available to a smaller number of children and was organized around a well-known religious figure. The core of the learning program consists of studying a book of prayers by means of constant drill and repetition.

Some children are able to attend regular schools in towns or larger villages. Two features are characteristic of these schools. First, schools often operate in shifts of unequal length, so that children attending the same school receive very different amounts of actual classroom learning ranging from eight to forty hours per week. The second characteristic feature is the size and composition of the class. Usually more than fifty students of different ages study together in one classroom. Promotion to the next class is based on the student's achievement rather than age. As a result, a great number of older but less advanced students stay in lower classes, while younger but more successful students climb up the school ladder at a rapid pace. The teaching methods are almost universally

based on frontal teaching (lecturing without feedback), continuous repetition, memorization, and drill. Problem-solving activities are limited,
even in mathematics. To solve a problem often means recalling the
correct solution of the same problem demonstrated by the teacher during the previous lesson. These seem to be the pervasive characteristics,
and deficiencies, of education in African countries. Cole and his colleagues (1971, p. 58) observed, "A great deal of learning that occurs can
hardly be characterized as problem solving in the usual sense, and it is
possible that learning capabilities are actually retarded by incoherent and
rigid instruction."

　Following their rapid and sometimes dramatic transition from
Ethiopia to their new home in Israel, immigrant children were confronted with educational settings and requirements that appeared unfamiliar and strange (Youth Aliyah, 1995). For a better understanding of
the specific educational problems of Ethiopian immigrants, one can
compare their experiences with those of another immigrant group, Russian Jews, who arrived in Israel during approximately the same period as
the Ethiopian group. By comparing the psychological and learning problems of these two groups, one can draw certain general conclusions
regarding the processes of educational acculturation.

　The first shock experienced by all new immigrants is associated
with the change of linguistic milieu. This shock, however, takes a very
different form in a group that comes from an oral culture, like the
Ethiopians, compared with a group from a modern literacy-based culture. For the Ethiopians, adaptation to a new linguistic milieu had two
aspects. The first aspect is related to the lack of compatibility between
their own learning practices and the Israeli educational approach to
teaching Hebrew as a second language. The Israeli system of Hebrew
instruction is based on a presumption of the students' literacy in their
native language. This presumption was certainly incorrect in regards to
the majority of the Ethiopian immigrants. Thus the task of second-language acquisition became compounded by the task of acquiring literacy
in an unknown language. The second aspect of linguistic adaptation
concerns the preservation and use of the student's native language and
the cultural tradition associated with it. Oral culture, by its very nature,
is largely dependent on specific social practices that ensure the transmission of oral knowledge and speech forms from generation to generation.
During long conversations over a cup of coffee Ethiopian adults retell

culturally significant stories, provide models for verbal riddles, and display a creative use of proverbs. Once such a practice is disrupted by the new social, economic, or geographical reality, the process of verbal and cultural transmission is in danger. For a person brought up in an oral culture there is no opportunity to turn to a book in order to reestablish an affinity with his or her native culture. Moreover, in the absence of texts that share in the Western literary tradition, immigrants from Ethiopia are left without those potential bridges that usually connect linguistically different but culturally interacting cultures such as the Russian and the Israeli.

Like the Ethiopians, Russian immigrants arrived in Israel without any previous experience with Hebrew and had to learn a language with a script different from both Russian and Latin. And yet their problems were not those of language acquisition per se, but the psychological problem of shifting from the language of Tolstoy and Dostoevsky, used by hundreds of millions of people, to a "minor" language with a limited literary tradition. The hyperliterate Russian immigrants, whose educational level was higher than that of native Israelis, resolved this problem by creating a number of Russian-language newspapers and magazines. This media served two goals: preserving the Russian-language culture and presenting the reality of Israeli life and culture in a familiar linguistic medium. Although a part of Russian culture became irrelevant in the Israeli context, a large enough segment of it, associated with the Western tradition in science, art, history, and literature, remained valuable. In simple terms, a Russian specialist in theoretical physics or in the history of the Roman Empire could continue existing in the same cultural space as before. Thus, somewhat paradoxically, the literary, text-based Russian culture demonstrated that it was less language dependent than the Ethiopian culture, based on oral tradition. The latter turned out to be singularly dependent on language-based meanings, the transmission of which hinged on the preservation of specific social practices.

Another important aspect of adaptation to a new culture involves the change in the position of the learner. As already noted, traditional Ethiopian learning is based on apprenticeship, imitation, and memorization. The student's own activity, initiative, and generalization from one type of a task to another is not particularly emphasized. The Israeli educational system, on the contrary, places considerable value on the student's own initiative, creativity, and, above all, ability to make the transfer from a demonstrated sample problem to a variety of other tasks. A distinctive feature of modern education is its process-oriented rather than product-oriented nature. It is not the product of the student's activity, be it a written text or a mathematical solution, that attracts pedagogical attention, but the processes leading to this or that product. The primary question is that of "how" rather than "what." This corresponds to the major focus of modern education, that is, the development in the student of an ability to become a true "agency," that is, an active source of his or her own learning activity. The student is expected to be able to generate all kinds of strategies leading to the desired outcome and to be conscious of the selection and construction of these strategies.

One of the most important tools of process-oriented education is problem solving. In traditional educational systems problem solving is only represented through mathematical problems, but modern education attempts to present almost any learning material in such a way that requires problem-solving activities. This poses a particular difficulty for all disadvantaged and educationally deprived students, immigrant students among them. Instead of simply calling for the memorization of the required material, or the recollection of previously given answers, the problem-solving activity requires a number of analytic steps.

First of all, in order to turn a task into a problem, a student should be able to detach it from his or her everyday experience. For example, the task of finding a missing word in the sentence "Sarah and Iris . . . not happy when they received new dresses as a present" has nothing to do with the everyday experience of immigrant students, who are happy to receive new dresses. Students should understand that the problem space here is grammatical, rather than pragmatic. By the same token, the task of comparing the characteristics of the shoreline of Greece with that of Libya does not presuppose the student's first-hand knowledge of these countries, but rather requires an ability to use maps or an encyclopedia for obtaining the necessary information. One may recall here Cole's (1990) claim that the problem solving of different cultural groups is context dependent. The point is, however, that one of the major aims of formal schooling is to prepare students for solving problems pertaining to new and unfamiliar contexts. The process-oriented nature of modern education calls for the development in students of problem-solving skills and strategies effective not only beyond their personal experiences, but also beyond the content material acquired in the classroom.

The central element of problem solving is the ability to see material as a problem. The task of finding the missing word in the sentence "Sarah and Iris . . . not happy when they received new dresses as a present" can be solved as a problem, but the same task can also be dealt with without resorting to problem-solving activity. A student may simply recall a similar expression, or insert "were" on the basis of simple association between using several names and "were." This kind of unproblematic approach is typical for a large number of students, and not merely immigrants or minority members. What distinguishes the problem-solving approach is a much more complex but at the same time fundamental treatment of any material as a potential problem. In the given example the method of turning it into a problem is to analyze the structure of the sentence, and on the basis of this analysis to identify that the missing word is a verb "to be," then to question tense and plurality, and to resolve this question using "when they received" as a cue. Only after this chain of analytic operations is constructed can a student confidently arrive at the answer, being aware not only of its correctness but also of the process by which the answer was selected.

Immigrant students whose previous educational experience is devoid of problem solving experience particular difficulties in working with tasks that require the spontaneous formulation of a problem and its subsequent resolution. They tend to rely on associations, recall, and other unproblematic approaches. Thus the task of teaching them how to see material as a problem becomes a special educational objective.

The above observation applies not only to students who have been deprived of regular formal education, but also to those who have received adequate instruction in basic skills but whose learning experience did not include the problem solving characteristic of contemporary Western education. Thus the often-used dichotomy of "unschooled" versus "schooled" individuals seems rather superficial. In the current debate on the role of schooling in cognitive development it is often emphasized that cross-cultural differences tend to disappear under the influence of systematic exposure to formal schooling (Cole, 1990). It is argued that children from so-called traditional societies who become exposed to formal education perform cognitive tasks on the same level as their peers in modern industrial societies. One may expect, therefore, a normative cognitive performance from culturally different adults who have accomplished a full course of school studies and become engaged in activities requiring school-based skills.

At the same time, pilot data on the learning skills of immigrants from Ethiopia who were high school graduates and who are enrolled at preparatory programs in Israeli universities indicate that these students lack some of the higher-order cognitive skills expected of their nonimmigrant peers (Inbal, 1985; August-Rothman and Zinn, 1986). My own observations of immigrant students also suggest that many of them have specific difficulties with the problem-solving situations that are typical of Western-type educational programs. These observations led to the hypothesis that cognitive development in many of the educated immigrants from Ethiopia occurred under conditions that included an adequate amount and type of mediated learning experience in their traditional culture but insufficient mediation of tools and strategies associated with Western-type education. Adequate mediation in the traditional culture created in them a good general learning potential. But the acquisition of tools and strategies associated with formal education had not been properly mediated to them. As a result reading, writing, and numerical, logical, and other symbolic activities remained in their minds as separate skills and failed to affect their overall cognitive functioning. The combination of overall good learning potential and specific difficulties related to the insufficient mediation of higher-order psychological tools and strategies created a condition amenable to relatively quick change in response to cognitive education intervention. It was thus hypothesized that (a) educated immigrants will demonstrate certain cognitive difficulties measurable by nonverbal cognitive assessment tests, and (b) they will respond positively to cognitive intervention in the form of the cognitive intervention program, and their cognitive difficulties will be alleviated as a result of intervention. Both of these hypotheses were confirmed (Kozulin and Lurie, 1994). A group of young adults who had completed more than twelve years of schooling in Ethiopia were tested by the Block Design subtest of the WISC-R battery and by Raven's Standard Progressive Matrices Test. The results of testing demonstrated an initial performance level significantly lower than is expected in educated adults. At the same time, cognitive intervention in the form of the Instrumental Enrichment program has led to a significant improvement of performance, thus confirming the hypothesis of the good general learning potential of this group.

## Specific Learning Difficulties Experienced by Immigrant Students

### Knowledge Base and Concepts

One of the most obvious but often ignored differences between immigrant students and their peers belonging to the majority culture is the difference in their knowledge base. With the almost universal involvement of younger Western children in some sort of preschool educational programs, these youngsters reach school with a considerable amount of general knowledge regarding objects and processes relevant to the learning process.

Twelve-year-old new immigrants from Ethiopia examined in a recent study (Kozulin et al., 1995), in contrast, demonstrated no knowledge of simple geometric figures such as a triangle and a square, failed to establish connections between observable objects such as stars in the sky and the graphic images of constellations, and experienced difficulty in comprehending that there is a fixed relationship between directions such as left, right, front, and back.

These students also demonstrated a somewhat narrow understanding of common concepts such as the notion of an error. By discussing with students the issue of errors made in problem-solving tasks the teacher discovered that the initial understanding of this concept was limited to spelling mistakes or arithmetical errors. Students failed to see the connection between arithmetical mistakes, mistakes made in other learning tasks, and errors made in everyday life. Special learning activities had to be constructed to show students that an error can occur in any situation when there is a deviation from the model or a correct solution. Students learned that errors can be classified along a number of parameters, such as errors of size, shape, color, quantity, time, and meaning. After appropriate cognitive intervention the students become capable of relating the concept of an error or a mistake to a variety of classroom and everyday life situations.

In the course of cognitive intervention special attention had to be paid to the formation in students of superordinate concepts such as size, form, color, origin, and use. Although the students easily distinguished between small and large objects, or objects of different colors, they initially experienced difficulty in subordinating this difference under the general notion of size or color. This finding does not imply that the Amharic language does not contain terms for superordinate concepts. The point is that superordinate terms known to Amharic-speaking students reflect the socially meaningful practices of their ethnic group, which do not necessarily coincide with those implied by the system of formal education. For example, the concept of "color" is much more abstract and universal in Hebrew or English than in Amharic, because it covers the color of all objects animate as well as inanimate. In Amharic this superordinate concept is less meaningful, because, for example, the color term "brown" used for the designation of the color of coffee cannot be used for describing the color of human skin and vice versa (Rosen, 1995). The concept of "depth" also cuts across different lines, because in Amharic the depth of a lake, the depth of a gorge, and the depth of a secret all require a different term for "depth." Similarly, the tone of a musical sound and the tone of the human voice cannot be subsumed under the common term "tone" because each requires a different word (Rosen, 1996).

The dominance of social practices can be best illustrated by the following vignette. I showed pictures of traditional Ethiopian musical instruments to a bright young man who had recently immigrated from Ethiopia. He confirmed his familiarity with all the instruments. When asked to group them, he immediately and confidently arranged them in groups of instruments that are played together and specified on what kind of social occasions each group of instruments is played. The suggestion to group them differently was not accepted as meaningful. For the informant there was no other way to group or define these instruments. For the Western observer these instruments could clearly be ordered into string instruments, wind instruments, and drums. Such a division is based on the superordinate concept of the "source of sound," which apparently was of minor importance in the context of Ethiopian cultural practices.

Certain notions essential for the analysis of all sorts of learning materials have had to be specially taught to immigrant students. One of them is the notion of degree of similarity. Many learning exercises in different content areas (geography, history, literature, and so on) require understanding the degree of similarity between a number of entities. For example, in asking a student whether the Israeli climate is more similar to the Egyptian or the English climate, the teacher usually presumes that the student already knows how to compare and only needs to acquire the necessary content information. However, this proved to be a wrong presupposition regarding immigrant students. At the beginning of their formal learning this task appeared to be difficult for them not because of their lack of knowledge regarding England and Egypt, but because of their difficulty with the establishment of the similarity procedure. The immigrant students had to acquire the notion of parameters of an object and their relative importance and then to form the notion of "distance" between a model object and each of the partially similar objects. Often such notions as degree of similarity are presumed to be self-evident and thus beyond the scope of school learning. Experience suggests that neglecting such notions may lead to distortions in the instructional process. Quite often new content information is provided to students who have not yet acquired conceptual tools for its proper analysis and comprehension. The above observations indicate that one cannot rely on the spontaneous accumulation of knowledge by immigrant and minority students. What appears as spontaneous learning in children from the cultural majority is often guided by tacit but powerful direction provided by their cultural environment, which accepts formal schooling as its "natural" part. These "spontaneously" acquired notions and the cognitive operations corresponding to them should thus be taught in an explicit and systematic way to immigrant students. Moreover, the curricular material should be constantly checked for the implicit notions and cognitive operations embedded in it.

## Graphic-Symbolic Devices

Contemporary learning materials employ a great variety of graphic-symbolic devices intended to facilitate the representation and manipulation of data. There is, however, nothing "natural" in such devices as tables, graphs, diagrams or plans. Their usefulness in conveying information is based on culturally specific conventions that must be learned. Without this prior learning they remain irrelevant and actually hinder students' understanding of the information they are purported to clarify. Special attention had to be paid to teaching Ethiopian immigrant students the rules of symbolization, leading from the real object to its "realistic" graphic image to its schematic rendition employing conventional signs. My experience with immigrant students suggests that the acquisition of graphic-symbolic devices and their internalization as information-processing and problem-solving tools should become a subject of special intervention.

The following graphic-symbolic devices are commonly used in contemporary schools, and their acquisition is a prerequisite for efficient work with learning materials:

*Signification, coding, and decoding,* including practice in the deliberate and arbitrary assignment of a chosen sign to an object or group of objects.

*Ordering and seriation,* including use of a numerical line for the placement of different quantities and use of columns for the seriation of values.

*Tables* as a combination of the principles of classification and seriation.

*Schemas and diagrams* as a means of demonstrating the relationships between the verbal description of a problem and its graphic representation.

*Plans and maps.*

*Graphs.* (Samples of exercises aimed at developing the student's facility to use graphic-symbolic devices can be found in Kozulin and Lurie 1997.)

*Signification, coding, and decoding* form the cornerstone of learning processes based on literacy in the broad sense of the word. One of the initial tasks of any schooling process is to teach younger students the correspondence between sounds or quantities and the arbitrary system of letters and numbers. The signification task is often presented to children in a narrow fashion only as a correspondence between the written and the spoken word and between the digit and the quantity it expresses. More advanced systems of signification such as mathematical, physical, and chemical formulae are introduced without special preparation. It is presumed that students are capable of spontaneously generalizing the rules of language and digit signification to other sign systems. This presupposition is justified, however, only for those sociocultural environments that in an informal way foster signification skills. The main point here is the ability of a student to grasp the arbitrary and deliberate nature of the signification process, which can put any sign in correspondence to any object or concept and then change the code if needed.

Many immigrant students experience specific difficulty while working with learning materials that contain a variety of signs. The main problem for them is to grasp the arbitrariness of the signification process. All traditional cultures have a rich system of signification and symbolization, so the basic act of connecting sign and meaning seems to be universal. In traditional cultures, however, the signification is imbedded in a concrete system of rituals and mytho-poetic narratives. What distinguishes the formal learning system is its emphasis on the radical arbitrariness of the sign–meaning connection. A student is expected to intuitively grasp this arbitrariness. For example, by placing the letters (a), (b), (c), . . . before each of a number of statements we do not imply any connection between these letters and the statements themselves. We simply code them for future manipulation as separate units of information. Moreover, we presume that one type of coding, for example, a letter code (a), (b), (c), can easily be changed into a different type of code, for example, (1), (2), (3). By introducing different codes we disregard some features of the coding devices that are meaningful in other contexts. For example, the a's in "all" and "All," which have a "natural" affinity when used as letters in words, lose this affinity when used as codes (a) and (A) for the enumeration of statements or the segments of a text. By coding the first statement (1) and the second statement (2) we use only the sequential meaning of digits but disregard their mathematical meaning. As a coding device (2) is not twice as big; it simply indicates a place after (1).

The situation becomes even more complicated when the "same" signs are used for different purposes within the same learning material. The letters (a), (b), (c), used for the enumeration of tasks, should be recognized as different from the same letters a × b × c, used as the "content" portion of an algebraic task.

To help students overcome these difficulties we developed a number of special exercises aimed at fostering signification skills. One of them is presented here; others can be found in Kozulin and Lurie (1997).

Let us create a secret code:
Letter a will be #

b    @
c    >
d    <
e    &
f    *

Using this code read the following words:
>  #  @
<  #  <
@  &  &  *

Using the code write the word: "face"
Can you write the word "code" using these signs?
For which letter do we need a code sign?
Create a code sign for this letter.
Now write the word "code":

*Ordering and seriation devices* constitute the next step following signification in the acquisition of grapho-symbolic tools. A student who has already mastered coding and decoding should now be able to symbolically arrange represented values in some order. Although Piaget (1969) considers successful seriation a marker of transition from preoperational to concrete-operational thinking, here the same type of operation is considered in conjunction with the acquisition of special tools that help students to master these operations. As in many other instances the Piagetian and Vygotskian approaches converge on the same phenomenon but from opposite sides. Piagetians perceive seriation as originating in children's spontaneous experimentation; it is seen as a cognitive operation that can be realized in different symbolic media. For Vygotskians, on the contrary, seriation appears as an end product of a systematically organized and symbolically mediated children's activity. Thus ordering and seriation devices are considered necessary tools for the development of seriation as a cognitive operation.

One of the most powerful seriation tools is a Number Line. It is important, however, not only that students acquire the technical skill to use the Number Line for seriation, but also that they realize that the qualitative result depends on the reference point and the question asked. The following seriation and ordering exercise provides an example of such diverse uses of the Number Line.

70___x___75_____80_____*_____90_____100____

1. The sign * indicates the place for number 84.
2. Which number can be at the place marked by (x)?
3. Find places for the numbers 78, 86, 91, 97.
4. Imagine that the numbers you found on the Number Line (78, 86, 91, 97) are results in a math test. Which result is the best? Which is the poorest?
5. Now imagine that the numbers you found on the Number Line are distances that different runners have to cover to reach the finish line. Which of the numbers shows the best position and which the worst one?
6. Imagine that the same numbers are numbers of bus lines. Can we say that one of them is better than another?

It is important that the qualitative results of tasks number 4 and number 5 be opposite, though the numbers involved are the same. This difference is associated with different reference points: in task number 4 the reference is 100, which is the best possible math test score; in task number 5 the reference point is 1, because it constitutes the minimum distance between the runner and the finish line. Task number 6 is introduced here in order to prevent possible overgeneralization. Students may assume that once some objects are expressed numerically, they should have an absolute positive or negative value like test results. The example of bus numbers helps to dispel this misconception.

*Schematic representations of problems and relationships* lie at the core of many modern learning materials. It is impossible to understand modern geography, economics, or physics textbooks without prior skill in decoding schemas, charts, and diagrams. At the same time there is a certain developmental paradox in the function of schematization. Many of young children's graphic representations bear signs of spontaneous schematization. Children's drawings often appear as schematic pictorial story representations rather than as realistic reproductions of objects. There is, however, no natural transition from the use of this spontaneous schematization to the deliberate system of schematization characteristic of academic learning materials. As with many other cognitive functions, the spontaneous schematization abilities of the child should be incorporated into and transformed by the new system of conventional and deliberate schematization. This transition becomes even more important in the case of immigrant students, who often have had limited opportunities for paper-and-pencil representational exercises in their previous learning.

The role of schematization in the learning process is so central because it fosters the function of abstraction and identification of the essential aspects of problems and relationships. When internalized, the function of schematization allows the student to work cognitively with only the essential elements of the task, leaving nonessential or circumstantial elements aside. On a more specific level, schematization exercises develop in the student an ability to translate verbal instructions or descriptions into the graphic-symbolic form, and to find a correspondence between different tasks that sound different but nevertheless express similar relationships.

The following is an example of one of such exercises that fosters students' ability to find a schematic form corresponding to the textual description.

Find out which schema in Figure 5.1 corresponds to the given problem. Abe had 15 candies. He ate 6 candies himself and

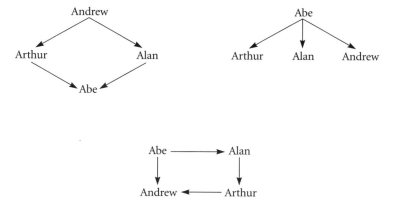

Figure 5.1  Schematic representation of a problem.

divided the rest equally between Arthur, Alan, and Andrew. How many candies did Alan receive?

## Cognitive Functions

One of the prime targets of cognitive intervention with ethnic minority and immigrant students is the development in them of the higher-order cognitive functions essential for successful formal learning. Teachers often take for granted the spontaneous development of many of these functions and as such they do not become a target of educational intervention. Frequently, however, these functions are poorly developed in immigrant students who lack previous educational experience, and thus should be formed in the course of specially designed learning activities.

The *ability to identify and define the problem* in the field of data is among the most important of these functions. Immigrant students with whom my colleagues and I worked experienced serious problems when confronted with the task of defining the problem in the absence of specific instructions or questions. They had to be taught that a problem can be implicit and that in order to discover it one should analyze the available data into what is given and what is not. Identification of a problem requires the student's activity in imposing certain cognitive schema on the available data. Despite their curiosity and strong motivation, immigrant students showed no aptitude for generating such cognitive schemas and had to be taught to form them in a course of specially designed activities.

For example, Figure 5.2 shows one of the exercises in which students are expected to identify the rule of the progression of numbers and fill in the missing numbers. The question is implicitly posed by the presence of empty spaces and an empty box above and between the numbers. Quite often such an implicit instruction was not recognized spontaneously, and required special analytic work that included identification of all elements of the task, forming hypotheses concerning the possible meaning of the empty spaces, and only after that arriving at the identification of the problem implicit in the picture.

Figure 5.2  Implicit question in the progression of numbers.

It was also important to develop in the students an understanding of the difference between the domain of a problem and the domain of possible answers, so that students could seek answers in the right domain. This function was particularly important in students' preparation for psychometric tasks, which often have perceptually similar questions and response domains. For example, students experienced difficulties in maintaining the separation between these domains on the page of a matrices test that had a number of tasks and a standard set of answers resembling the tasks (Figure 5.3 schematically shows the problem and response domains in the tasks based on Raven's Matrices).

Another important cognitive function developed in the course of cognitive intervention was the *ability to work with several sources of information*. Our students were baffled in the beginning by tasks that required coordination of the information provided by written instructions, model objects, and written specifications. In one of the Instrumental Enrichment tasks (Figure 5.4) students had to generate figures similar to the model only in terms of certain parameters (for example, form and number), with the implication that they could differ from the model in all other respects. It was necessary to introduce students to the notion of the universe of the model's parameters, further divided into those fixed by

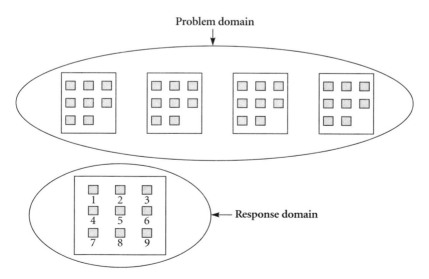

Figure 5.3 Problem and response domains in a matrix task.

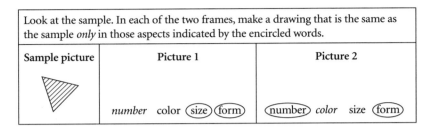

Look at the sample. In each of the two frames, make a drawing that is the same as the sample *only* in those aspects indicated by the encircled words.

| Sample picture | Picture 1 | Picture 2 |
|---|---|---|
| | *number* color ⬭size⬭ ⬭form⬭ | ⬭number⬭ *color* size ⬭form⬭ |

Figure 5.4 Instrumental Enrichment—"Comparisons." (Arlington Heights, Ill.: IRI/Skylight, 1996, © R. Feuerstein, HWCRI.)

the written specifications task and those open to change as implied in the written instructions. The crucial moment was in the integration of all these sources of information in the form of a generated response figure.

In certain cases the students showed a more general difficulty in integration, that is, an inability to integrate separate learning experiences into coherent schema allowing for the progressive mastery of material. This necessitated special work aimed at integrating already acquired knowledge, skills, and strategies into cognitive units and demonstrating their applicability to currently studied material.

Probably the most significant of achievements in the field of cognitive functions was the immigrant students' gradual mastery of *planning* their own problem-solving actions. Planning is important because it promotes the students' metacognitive understanding of their own cognitive activity. Instead of choosing the answer in an intuitive and undifferentiated way, the students are taught to reflect upon their own actions, control these actions, and evaluate their outcome. As a result the students become conscious of their own learning activity and capable of organizing it according to a clearly developed plan. One of the most complicated aspects here is the realization that alternative planning may lead to equally satisfactory results. Our students experienced particular difficulty understanding alternative planning; this difficulty has not been overcome completely.

### Language and Communication

The immigrant students we worked with demonstrated a disparity, typical in language acquisition, between a relatively quick and successful

acquisition of communicative speech in Hebrew and protracted problems with the comprehension of abstract concepts and their hierarchical
organization. Such a disparity appears to be quite typical for immigrants
who lack formal educational background (Cummins, 1989). This disparity may also reflect the predominant model of teaching Hebrew as a
second language, which places a major emphasis on social communication rather than on verbal thinking. Such a teaching model largely ig-
nores the important difference between oral and literate language. This
difference and its educational consequences were identified by Vygotsky
(1986) and currently stimulate an intense debate (Olson and Torrance,
1991). It is important to recognize that as reading is more than just a
decoding skill, writing is more than a skill of encoding oral messages in
a sign form. Literacy is not a technical skill, but a particular cognitive and
psychological attitude. Although oral exchanges are mostly contextual,
the use of texts both presupposes and enhances decontexualization, or,
more precisely, texts increasingly serve as contexts for other texts.

The oral tradition in which our students were brought up is richly
contextual and integrative. This means that the speaker is relying on an
immediately shared social and cultural horizon of interlocutors and
integrates different domains into one thought/speech unit. Such an orientation works quite successfully for second-language acquisition as
long as the goal is here-and-now communication about issues at hand.
Formal learning, however, requires both greater differentiation within
the thought/speech unit and, in particular, greater decontexualization.
Text-based speech is decontextualized because its aim is to provide
self-contained information for people who lead lives different from
one's own.

It is not enough, however, to acquire literacy as a technical skill. As
shown in a number of studies (Cole et al., 1971; Goody, 1987), literacy
in and by itself rarely leads to significant changes in learning and cognitive style. What is essential is those practices and uses in which literacy is
involved. In his analysis of Indian literacy Narasimhan (1991, p. 179) has
argued:

> Indian tradition, in the large, continued to remain an oral one
> in its psychosocial aspects. There was no effort to discriminate
> between myth and history, between beliefs in the supernatural
> and a rational analysis of natural phenomena; between disputa-
> tions, polemical arguments, and comparative, critical, analytic

studies; between a didactic approach to inquiry and a reflective approach to it . . . It would appear that what is of relevance is not the existence of a textual tradition per se but the kinds of conceptualizations and critical analytical techniques such a tradition develops and makes use of in textual studies.

What is true for the consequences of literacy on the societal level can also be true on the individual level. It is not enough to make students formally literate; one should also engage them in such uses of literacy that are relevant for the goal of formal education. Literacy in this broader sense seems to be influential in terms of separating factual information from its various interpretations and in promoting metacognitive awareness (Olson, 1991).

Acquisition of literacy by bilingual students is often complicated by our views regarding bilingualism as such (Valdes and Figueroa, 1994). One of the primary misconceptions is a belief that each human individual has a native language, which serves as a natural basis for second-language acquisition: "We may conjecture that every speaking human is a native speaker of a language. This is not true either, as results from bilingualism studies show. The typical case is that bilinguals are not native speakers of either language. Moreover there are those people who have forgotten their native language for various reasons, e.g. because of living abroad in an environment linguistically different from the native one. Hence, the implication from speaking human being to native speaker does not hold" (Ballmer, 1981, pp. 54–55).

When speaking about second-language acquisition in immigrant students we often tend to forget that their first language may be "incomplete," at least in the sense that they come from an oral culture and lack literacy in their native language. Apart from its communicative role, language has a major cognitive role as an instrument of reasoning. The development of verbal reasoning in the second language, especially when the first one is oral, is a daunting task. Cognitive intervention helps to create general cognitive prerequisites essential for the successful development of a second language as an instrument of learning and reasoning. Certain essential concepts and their relationships can be introduced in the course of cognitive intervention programs. These cognitive lessons, however, cannot substitute for the systematic teaching of language as a tool of reasoning. Difficulties observed in immigrant students call for a new approach in teaching language to similar populations of students. This approach should combine teaching how to communicate and how to decode written text with greater emphasis on verbal concepts, cognitive aspects of text comprehension, and the development of verbal reasoning. The first step in this direction has been made in a series of English workbooks for black South African students (Wallace, Pandaram, and Modiroa, 1996) that emphasize the cognitive aspects of second-language acquisition.

## Inducing Cognitive Change in Immigrant Students

My colleagues and I conducted a study investigating conditions inducing cognitive change in adolescent immigrants from Ethiopia who were integrated into the Israeli educational system. From previous studies with similar populations of immigrant students (Greenberg and Kaniel, 1990; Kaniel et al., 1991), it became clear that they possess high learning potential, which, however, often fails to express itself in actual school performance because of the students' cultural difference and lack of experience with formal learning. We reasoned that the Instrumental Enrichment (IE) cognitive intervention program (Feuerstein et al., 1980), which was designed to create cognitive prerequisites of learning and develop learning strategies in disadvantaged students, might play a decisive role in inducing the needed cognitive change (cf. Skuy et al., 1994, 1995). The occurrence and magnitude of cognitive change was assessed through pre- and post-testing students using Raven's Standard Progressive Matrices (Raven, 1960).

### Participants

The participants in this study belonged to a group of immigrant adolescent girls from Ethiopia studying in an Israeli boarding school. Fifteen of these students were present at both the pretest and the post-test and received a full amount of IE cognitive intervention. All the participants immigrated to Israel in May-June 1991 during the mass exodus of Ethiopian Jewry known as "Operation Shlomo." At the time of arrival their mean age was 11.5. One should be aware, however, that since the new immigrants possessed no documentation confirming their birth dates, their age was established only very approximately. Among the fifteen participants two claimed that they had attended village schools in Ethiopia for a period of approximately three years, three claimed participation in reading programs for a period of half a year, and the rest had no experience whatsoever with formal learning.

Upon their arrival in Israel all participants were placed in intensive Hebrew study classes *(ulpan)* for a period ranging from three to six months. After that half of them were directed to the boarding school where the present study later took place. The other half of the participants initially went through a number of schools where they studied in integrated classes and in classes specially created for the new immigrants. At the beginning of the 1993–94 school year all participants were concentrated in special classes for immigrant students at the boarding school already mentioned. Their families had settled in different parts of the country, approximately half of them in temporary trailer parks populated almost exclusively by new immigrants. Participants visited their families once every two weeks and during vacations. Little is known about parental involvement in the students' lives. It is significant, however, that only in one case did school teachers mention parental involvement and support of a daughter's studies.

### Cognitive Intervention and Cognitive Change

The IE intervention program began in October 1993 and continued for two school years. On average students received 4 hours of IE per week, for a total of 220 hours. The following IE instruments were taught: "Organization of Dots," "Orientation in Space I & III," "Analytic Perception," "Comparisons," and selected pages from "Illustrations." An important element of IE teaching is the "bridging" exercises that link principles acquired in the course of an IE lesson to the tasks of content lessons and everyday life experiences. The philosophy and goals of IE intervention were explained to the school administration and content subject teachers, who were in constant contact with the IE teacher.

Assessment of cognitive change in the participants was undertaken using Raven's Standard Progressive Matrices (RSPM) as a cognitive measure. The participants were pretested in November 1993, approxi-

*Table 5.1* Raven Standard Progessive Matrices (RSPM) pretest and post-test scores and standard deviations ($N = 15$)

|  | Pretest | Post-test | $t$ | $p$ |
|---|---|---|---|---|
| RSPM score | 29.20 (9.43) | 43.67 (9.06) | 4.29 | 0.001 |

mately one month after the beginning of the IE intervention program, and post-tested in March 1995. Between the pretest and post-test the participants received no exposure to RSPM and no coaching in psychometric test taking.

The data presented in Table 5.1 demonstrate dramatic and statistically significant improvement in the participants' RSPM scores from the pre- to the post-test. Table 5.2 contains data on five RSPM items, B8–B12. These items were selected for special analysis because their correct solution requires analogical reasoning. Since analogical reasoning constitutes one of the fundamental prerequisites of successful formal learning, it was important to ascertain the emergence of cognitive change in this area. If at the beginning of the program the students could, on average, solve only 41 percent of the analogy tasks correctly, after the IE intervention their success rate reached 79 percent.

Table 5.3 and Figure 5.5 provide a comparison between the participants in the IE intervention program and a matching group of new immigrants from Ethiopia who received no IE intervention. The members of the non-IE group were matched to the participants in the IE program in terms of their age, time of immigration to Israel, school type, and educational experiences in Israel. The non-IE group was tested in February 1995. There is a significant difference between the RSPM scores of the IE group and the non-IE group, while no difference is observed between the IE group and the Israeli norm for ages 14+. One may

*Table 5.2* Pretest and post-test scores and standard deviations for five RSPM items B8–B12 ($N = 15$)

|  | Pretest | Post-test | $t$ | $p$ |
|---|---|---|---|---|
| Items B8–B12 | 2.07 (1.83) | 3.93 (1.34) | 3.19 | 0.01 |

*Table 5.3*  RSPM scores and standard deviations for the IE intervention group
(*N* = 15), matching non-IE group of immigrant adolescents (*N* = 17),
and Israeli norms for age 14+

|            | IE group  |              |              |
|------------|-----------|--------------|--------------|
| Pretest    | Post-test | Non-IE group | Israeli norm |
| 29.20      | 43.67     | 29.3         | 45.46        |
| (9.43)     | (9.06)    | (12.5)       | (8.25)       |

IE-group (post-test) versus non-IE group: $t$ = 3.75; $p$ < 0.01.
IE-group (post-test) versus Israeli norm: not significant.

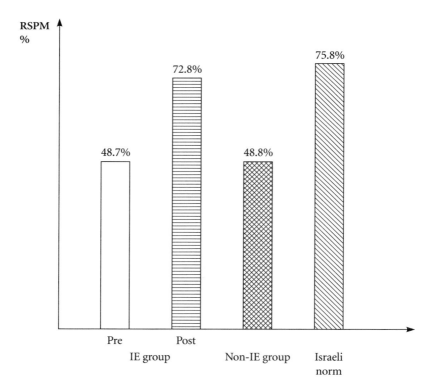

Figure 5.5  Raven Standard Progressive Matrices scores (in percent) for the IE intervention group, the matching non-IE group, and the Israeli norm for age 14+.

conclude that mere exposure to formal school education as experienced by the members of the non-IE group failed to produce in them the cognitive change that was successfully induced in the members of the IE group. It is also significant that a two-year IE intervention was sufficient to bring participants' RSPM scores to the level of their veteran Israeli peers.

## Conclusion

The difficulties experienced by immigrant students indicate that cross-cultural differences in cognition are most probably related to learning practices characteristic of different cultures and subcultures. These differences can be observed not only between cultures but also within a given culture, depending on specific learning patterns predominant in a subgroup of learners. It should be recognized that school-based formal learning is not a mere extension of everyday experience; it requires a special approach to learning material, special uses of language, and special forms of problem solving. With respect to the mainstream majority culture, many of the cognitive prerequisites of school-based learning are formed in the child in the course of "spontaneous" (actually, tacitly guided) interactions with parents, peers, and other carriers of their culture. It would be incorrect to assume that the same process occurs equally "spontaneously" in the immigrant and minority students who lack the environment conducive to developing these prerequisites.

Two major determinants of cognitive prerequisites are conceptual literacy and facility with other symbolic psychological tools, and a mediated learning experience responsible for the integration of these tools into the cognitive system of the student. Both psychological tools and mediated learning acquisitions do not occur spontaneously and should be organized and carried out in a systematic way. Thus the major emphasis in the education of minority students should be on the development of learning strategies, metacognitive functions, and conceptual literacy. Only when these prerequisites are in place can one expect the minority student to succeed in the acquisition of new content material.

# 6 ❦

# Literature as a Psychological Tool

In sociocultural psychology culture is considered to be the very fabric of human experience. Accordingly, human activity aimed at the creation and interpretation of culturally significant phenomena should be accepted as paradigmatic. Within this paradigm, literature plays a particularly important role. On the one hand, the composition of a literary text constitutes one of the most advanced forms of psychological activity; on the other hand, a literary text is a psychological supertool that mediates human experience. The literary model for psychology proposed here, therefore, has two complementary goals. One of them is to inquire into human psychological life as "authoring" *in potentia*. The other is to investigate the role of internalized literary modalities as mediators of human experience. These two possibilities will be illustrated by the analysis of the relative contribution of decontextualized thinking and intertextually rich discourse to cognitive maturity, and in the use of a higher-order psychological tool such as a whole literary work as an instrument of cognitive change.

## Natural-Scientific versus Cultural Psychology

Psychology has long been faulted for being an "inexact" science. Such criticism is provoked by the disparity between psychology's actual performance and its continuing insistence on the scientific character of its methods and findings. Although the poor record of psychology as an exact science is well documented (Koch, 1981; Sarason, 1981), alternative models of self-identification are in short supply. As soon as the scientific identity of psychology is questioned, the unpleasant ghost of armchair psychology based on introspective self-observation makes its appearance and scares psychologists back into the scientific province.

Only recently and with considerable hesitation have American psychologists begun to entertain the idea of a closer alliance with the humanities (for example, Sarbin, 1986; Bruner, 1986; Polkinghorne, 1988; Stigler, Shweder, and Herdt, 1990; see also Smith, Harre, and Langenhove, 1995). This still barely visible movement has been triggered, on the negative side, by the limitations of the natural-scientific method as applied to human psychology and, on the positive side, by the spectacular strides made in recent decades by philology, linguistics, and cultural anthropology. It should also be mentioned that the cultural psychological approach has been practiced de facto by some professionals and academics who exist on the institutional fringes of establishment psychology (in, for example, schools of education, departments of linguistics, and reading programs). Their work, however, is not reflected in the standard lore of psychology textbooks and licensing exams.

The pivotal moment in psychology's reorientation toward the humanities occurs when it changes its stance toward the categories of nature and culture. Scientific psychology sometimes explicitly, but more often tacitly, assumes that culture is a superstructure of human existence whose foundations are of a biological character. Culture therefore can be included in the scientific psychological equation as a form of human environment, or an external requirement imposed on human behavior. To understand behavior or cognition scientifically means to be able to "bracket" the multiplicity of culturally dependent appearances and to identify the underlying natural mechanisms. Only when this has been achieved can one begin to discuss the so-called ecological validity of the obtained data.

In contrast, in psychology that is patterned after the humanities, culture is considered to be the foundation of human experience. It is presumed that the transition from biological evolution to human history radically changed the psychological equation, so that culture became the true "nature" of the human world. From this point of view the authentic form of human existence is "being in culture." Accordingly, the creation and interpretation of culturally significant phenomena becomes the primary behavioral and cognitive research (Geertz, 1973).

An early attempt to reform psychological theory along these lines was made by Vygotsky (1978, 1986, 1987; Vygotsky and Luria, 1993; see also Kozulin, 1990a), who emphasized that higher mental processes emerge out of human activity mediated by the "psychological tools" of semiotic character. Cognitive development therefore appears to be dependent on the progressive mastery of ever more complex systems of symbolic mediators. Language, writing, and different literary forms are those cultural-psychological tools that provide the formal mechanism for human mastery of psychological processes. It is important to emphasize that semiotic systems and literature in particular are taken here in their formal aspect, as semiotic devices, and not as a body of images or ideas. The word "formal" stands for such aspects of discourse as its genre-specificity, the ability to encompass temporary relationships, the hypothetical, "as if" possibilities inherent in it, and so on. Thus we are not going to discuss how the content of a literary work affects human cognition, but rather how cognition is affected by the possibilities inherent in literary form. Literature may serve both as a prototype of the most advanced forms of human psychological life and as a concrete "psychological tool" mediating human experience. Cultural psychology therefore has two complementary goals. One of them is to inquire into human psychological life, understood as "authoring" *in potentia.* The other is to investigate the role of internalized literary modalities as mediators of human experience.

The different positions of scientific and cultural psychology vis-à-vis nature and culture are "translated" into different methodological attitudes. The attitude of scientific psychology is derived from scientific epistemology developed since the seventeenth century. Natural-scientific epistemology reflects a special kind of cognitive and physical practice that allows for the creation of artificial conditions under which the plane of theoretical representations can be put into correspondence with the plane of physical (or psychological) manipulation of the object of inquiry. This practice, known as a "scientific experiment," is organized in such a way that the characteristics discovered in the object under study are independent of the procedures involved. Moreover, the laws of the behavior of the object are deemed to be truly objective only if they are not affected by either the method of experimentation or the fact of experimentation itself.

It has been argued that even the most rigorous of psychological experiments cannot comply with the requirements of the scientific model because of the essentially interactive character of any psychological situation (Friedman, 1967). Moreover, the very existence of the processes studied by psychology often depends on irreversible changes occurring in the mental operations of the individual. Learning processes, for example, can often be studied only in the framework of a "formative experiment." During such an "experiment" certain learning capacities are generated in a child that were absent before and that will not emerge unless the child is engaged in "experimental" activity. In a sense, any study of creative cognition changes the mode of the mind's operation in such a way that it cannot return to its original state. By the same token any psychotherapeutic encounter is such an "experimental" situation, during which the processes in the client's mind can be studied only because they are irreversibly changed.

In cultural psychology this creative, emergent character of the human mind is accepted as its most important aspect. Consequently both the subject matter of psychology and its methods are modified. In what concerns the subject matter, culturally intensive processes such as the creation or interpretation of cultural texts should take precedence over purely adaptive, quasi-biological processes. For example, rather than approaching the problem of memory from the point of view of abstractive mechanisms of retention and the retrieval of artificial stimuli, it can be approached in terms of the integration of disjointed episodes of human life into a coherent narrative whole. The paradigmatic case for this type of memory would be a literary re-creation of a given character's entire life. In the course of its long history literature has accumulated a wealth of techniques for creating the aesthetically "rounded," completed lives of characters. Some of these techniques are employed, without being recognized, beyond the realm of literature. For example, the child's early autobiographic memory is substantially influenced by the ordering devices supplied by adults in the form of narratives (often resembling short stories) about the child's early years (Halbwachs, 1980). Any culturally meaningful activity can serve as a source of knowledge about human psychological life. Apparently Vygotsky had this in mind when he wrote that "every poem is a little experiment—a snare for psychological functions" (Vygotsky, 1982, p. 406).

A possible solution to the perpetual crisis in twentieth-century psychology would be, therefore, to acknowledge psychology's alliance with the humanities, and to conceive it as a systematic form of cultural knowledge. Ontologically such psychology should be grounded in culture (versus nature), epistemologically it should be concerned with interpretation (versus prediction), and methodologically it should be oriented toward semiotics (versus physics).

At the same time care should be taken to distinguish the province of cultural psychology from that of the humanities proper. The distinction, however, can be elaborated only in the process of transcending the limits of traditional psychology and trespassing into the field of humanities. The province of cultural psychology can be defined as a "territory" separating the individual intention toward a culturally meaningful act and the objectivized result of such an act, which is the proper subject for linguistics, poetics, logic, and so on.

## Two Faces of Psychoanalysis

The clear predominance of natural-scientific methodology in twentieth-century psychology does not imply, however, that psychologists have always been consistent in their adherence to the scientific model. The potential ambivalence of psychology's position is nowhere as apparent as in the history of psychoanalysis. Psychoanalysis as a theory and as a practice reveals a deep and significant schism between two coexisting models—the humanistic and the mechanistic. This schism can be traced to the original ambivalence of Freud's position. On the one hand, Freud's clinical method is based on the interpretation of the meaning of the patient's speech, dreams, and other symptoms. Analytic treatment is essentially the restoration of the distorted meaning carried out in the medium of the spoken word, hence the term "talking cure." This aspect of psychoanalysis allows one to interpret it as a special case of semiotic analysis, which has been the position of some French authors for quite some time (Barthes, 1982). Moreover, the intellectual sources of Freud's doctrine include literary works and mythological stories. As Freud himself once admitted, the essential themes of his theories were based on the intuition of poets (Ellenberger, 1970, p. 460). This compelled even the more scientistic of Freud's followers to admit that "man [for Freud] is a producer and processor of subjective meanings, by which he defines himself; and one of his strongest needs is to make his life meaningful. It is implicit in the humanistic image that meanings are primary, irreducible, causally efficacious, and of complete dignity as a subject of systematic interest" (Holt, 1972, p. 9).

On the other hand Freudian metapsychology, which is based on the principles of mental topography and economy, has a clear natural-scientific orientation. Its dependence on the nineteenth-century concept of scientific knowledge is well documented (Sulloway, 1979) as well as its conflict with the humanistic attitude. "The metapsychological language constantly points us away from real human beings, their concrete sufferings and aspirations, and invites us to see instead a bloodless battle of ego, superego, and id, anticathexis being pitted against cathexis, energies being fused, neutralized and what not, while structures interact with objects, and real people disappear behind the impressive cloud of words" (Holt, 1972, p. 14). The prestige of the scientific model is, however, so strong that the same Holt who criticized Freud's mechanistic approach was ready to claim that the humanities have no method of their own. He assured his readers that he had "examined the methods used in such humanistic disciplines as literary criticism and history" and concluded that "to the extent that they are disciplined—these methods are substantially identical with those of science" (Holt, 1972, p. 19). Still there remains an undeniable gap between psychoanalytic practice, which is "humanistic" by definition, and psychoanalytic theory, which stubbornly aspires to be scientific. Holzman (1976, pp. 134–135) remarked that clinical psychoanalysis "developed as an interpretative discipline, the one with a great concern for 'meaning,' but adopted for the theory not the clinical theory but the physicalist language of energy, forces, and counterforces."

The inner intellectual ambivalence of psychoanalysis also seems to have an overt professional-institutional counterpart. The psychoanalyst, as conceived of by Freud, was a layperson with, presumably, a broadly based humanistic education. The reality of the development of psychoanalysis in the United States, however, has made a psychoanalyst almost invariably the holder of an M.D. degree. Patients seem ready to entrust themselves only to professionals with solid medical-biological backgrounds, although the methods of treatment these professionals are using have nothing to do with scientific medicine. On the part of the psychoanalyst the ambivalence is also obvious. The actual practice of psychoanalysis puts a strong demand on cultural knowledge and psychological intuition, but at the same time the very ability to practice depends on the analysts' compliance with institutionalized medical-scientific requirements. Even as a form of discourse psychoanalysis has displayed a remarkable ambivalence, insisting on the scientistic lexicon of forces and drives and at the same time developing an elegant literary style that has nothing to do with the prose of scientific papers.

## Life as Authoring

Psychology, following the lead of the literary model, has two major directions. One of them can be called a life as authoring approach. Within this perspective the entire range of human conduct is perceived as analogous to the process of authoring. Human thoughts, acts, and intentions can be viewed as authoring, and the emerging self can be viewed as an artifact analogous to the author of the literary work. As language is potential literature, human conduct can also be conceived of as a potential text. At the same time, if we take into account the paramount position of the production of texts among the human psychological processes, its study can be taken as a paradigm for the study of other psychological processes (Kozulin, 1991). In both cases, the boundary between "artificial" (art and literature) and "natural" (individual psychology) is removed. Literary work becomes a model for the reconstruction of the emergence of the human self, while specific rules of literary discourse inform our understanding of the narrative thinking of the individual (Bruner, 1986).

The life as authoring approach is based on the ideas of the Russian philosopher and philologist Mikhail Bakhtin (1986, 1990; see also Clark and Holquist, 1984; Wertsch, 1991). While in the natural sciences the primary given is an object, and what is sought is the causal explanation of its behavior, in humanities the primary given is the text, and what is sought is its meaning. "The text (written or oral) is the primary given of all those disciplines and of all thought on the human sciences . . . The text is the unmediated reality (reality of thought and experience), the only one from which those disciplines and this thought can emerge. Where there is no text, there is no object of study, and no object of thought either" (Bakhtin, 1986, p. 103).

The natural-scientific approach to human behavior attempts to derive even the highest forms of human conduct from the elementary, preverbal cognitive and behavioral processes with respect to which language is more or less a passive system of labeling. The principles of cultural psychology, on the contrary, suggest that the most trivial of everyday dialogues contains in itself a nucleus of human language as a whole, which in its turn finds its ultimate embodiment and realization in literature. Language therefore is neither a mere accompaniment of actions nor a simple medium of expression for ideas; it is a tool for turning this reality from a "given" into something that is "developing." Language helps to discern the higher, creative potential in the "lower" forms of psychological life. Language thus offers a paradigm for any action that involves interaction or interpretation.

Contemporary semiotics has incorporated the nonverbal phenomena of everyday life into the sphere of cultural-semiotic interpretation (Greimas, 1987). For example, what from the point of view of psychophysiology would appear as a sensory-motor activity, and from the cognitive point of view as a mental schema or script, in the cultural-semiotic perspective becomes a gestural program. Any sensory-motor activity approached from the point of view of its cultural meaning becomes a "gesture" or a chain of "gestures." Thus a gestural program such as "sewing a dress" can be understood as a genetic definition of a particular thing, a dress. A dress thus becomes a "message," an embodied gesture of one person addressed to another. A dress as an object, as a piece of cloth can, at best, be psychologically interpreted as a "stimulus." The same dress understood as an end product of a gestural program has a much richer psychological content. For example, there are profoundly different psychological connotations for "hand-sewn" dresses and "machine-sewn" dresses. Once cultural objects are produced, they become elements of other gestural programs, for example, "putting on a new dress" or "taking off" a dress. It is significant that literary texts provide a far more detailed analysis of the psychological dimension of different gestural programs than scientific psychology does.

Bakhtin's (1990) analysis of the relationships among the author, the literary hero, and the artistic text as a whole provides insight into the possibilities of the "life as authoring" approach. According to Bakhtin, the author does not coincide with any of the aspects of his (or her) life or writing but reveals himself only in the totality of the literary work. In a similar way the self cannot be reduced to any of the here-and-now characteristics of its life. It would be erroneous to seek the answers to the phenomenon of authoring in the personality of a particular writer, as psychoanalysis has done more than once (Natoli and Rusch, 1984). Indeed, it is important to understand that the personality of a particular writer does not coincide with his or her essence as an author. But the author is not one of the characters either, even in first-person narratives. The author is present in the text, and emerges only from the text, but at the same time he cannot be located in this text as a singular figure. "Just as the self can never be completely imagined as a person like other persons, so the author can never be fully perceived as another person. The reason for the invisibility of the author is the same as that for the invisibility of the self: The author is not a single fixed entity so much as a capacity, an energy" (Clark and Holquist, 1984, p. 88).

One of the primary literary models for the construction of a self is that of an autobiography. Long neglected by psychologists, the genre of autobiography has only recently, and not without the influence of Bakhtin, emerged as a possible avenue for the study of narrative thinking. "The heart of my argument is this," wrote Bruner. "Eventually the culturally shaped cognitive and linguistic processes that guide the self-telling of life narratives achieve the power to structure perceptual experience, to organize memory, to segment and purpose-build the very 'events' of the life. In the end, we become the autobiographic narratives by which we 'tell about' our lives" (Bruner, 1987, p. 15).

The analysis of autobiography as a literary genre not only supplies us with a model of the "construction" of the self, but also helps to discern the boundary between psychological and aesthetic self-reflection. Relevant to this topic Bakhtin (1990) made an important observation regarding the "surplus of vision" of the author. When writing from the point of view of one of the characters, the author "lives into" this character's horizon. But then at a certain moment in the creative process the author "returns" to his own privileged position and supplements what was visible for the chosen character by other perceptions. Only through this surplus of vision is the author capable of presenting the life of a chosen character as a complete one, as aesthetically finished. In autobiographical writing this "return" is denied, because the writer does not have any surplus of vision in respect to himself. Autobiography as an art form compels the author to remain within the horizon of a chosen character through the eyes of whom the writer's life may appear as aesthetically finished. Here we can discern the border between literature as a paradigm for psychological life and literature as a self-important aesthetic phenomenon. In real life, for example, in the nonliterary autobiographic narrative, the individual usually "returns" to his own privileged position that dominates the perception of others. And since the self is open to change while alive, the autobiographic narrative remains a personal document rather than a work of art. Aesthetic completeness is not ordinarily the aim of an individual, and thus he sacrifices it in order to have the "last word" in the tale of his own life.

Beyond the genre of autobiography, literature also suggests special types of relationships between the author and the character. The real-life analogues of these relationships sometimes manifest themselves as pathologies. One of them is the denial of the authorial privileged position by the character. The character promotes his own point of view, which is not encompassed by that of the author. The character also is not properly integrated into the general "scenery" of the book. According to Bakhtin (1973), this type of relationship is characteristic of many of Dostoyevsky's and Tolstoy's characters. In the plane of psychological life a somewhat analogous process occurs when a person loses or surrenders his or her surplus of vision and becomes confined to the horizons of others without encompassing them. Such a person speaks using the voices of others, but fails to develop his own authoritative position. The opposite pathology appears in the case of extreme narcissism when the author (self) forces his or her point of view on others, turning them into marionettes. The independent horizons of the others are ignored and substituted for by the egocentric vision of the self. The self's "return" in this case would be an illusion, because others serve only as props for his own vision.

The author's surplus of vision also allows for the temporal encompassing of the lives of the characters. The individual cannot experience his own life as temporally finished and aesthetically accomplished, if only because the individual does not have the experience of the beginning and the end of his life. The beginning always appears as a "story" told by others, and the end also, but as a constantly changing "story" imagined by the individual himself. The life of a character, or a real other, can on the contrary be seen as an accomplished whole. Our surplus of vision in respect to others allows us to construct a complete "story" of their lives, to turn these lives from a sequence of disjointed experiences into the whole of memory. Memory about the other is essentially different from reminiscences and contemplation about one's own life. Only the life of the other taken in its totality can become a subject for the value judgment that goes beyond the aims and meanings held by the person while he was alive. Building one's memory of the other is probably the most aesthetically intensive practice available in everyday life.

Thus the first tentative implication of cultural psychology for education is that more attention should be paid to the literary creative process as a paradigm of human understanding. Literature should be used not only as a source of information, images, and ideas but also as a specific method of representation and thinking.

### Autonomous Text versus Intertextuality

As noted earlier, the task of cultural psychology involves not only promoting a paradigm of literary action but also inquiring into culturally intensive human activities. One of the issues that the cultural psychological approach may clarify is the problem of the so-called autonomous text. The notion of autonomous text was introduced into psychology and education by Olson (1977). Olson suggested that in autonomous text meaning is explicitly and unambiguously expressed in words and syntactic patterns. In contrast, an "utterance" is contextual and ambiguous. The problem of "texts" versus "utterances" has both academic and social implications. As a social problem it plays a significant role in the debate regarding power and authority as linked with formal literacy and in the opposition between oral and written traditions (Gee, 1986, 1990). On the academic side, Olson's (1977) thesis about the cultural and developmental superiority of written "autonomous" text over oral contextual speech has become a standard point of reference. "My argument," Olson wrote, "will be that there is a transition from utterance to text both culturally and developmentally and that this transition can be described as one of increasing explicitness, with language increasingly able to stand as an unambiguous or autonomous representation of meaning" (p. 258).

The evolution of human verbal cognition both historically and ontogenetically proceeds from context-dependent oral utterances to autonomous texts, of which scientific papers are the most advanced examples. Scientific text represents "the truth of correspondence" between statements and empirical observations. This truth of correspondence should be distinguished from the "truth of wisdom" that is perpetuated in oral and poetic traditions, and which apparently retains its contextual character (Olson 1977, p. 277).

Although there is much truth in what Olson says about the cognitive consequences of writing, both his choice of scientific writing as a telos of language development and his definition of the autonomous text are far from convincing. Above all, the whole issue of the decontextualization of verbal thought is not a simple one. Although the progression from context-dependent actions and verbal utterances to decontextualized mental operations was established in developmental psychology long ago (Werner, 1948; Werner and Kaplan, 1963), this progression is apparently accompanied by yet another process. This is the process of the ever-increasing role of intralinguistic relations in the child's thinking (Wertsch, 1985a, pp. 145–157). Intralinguistic devices can be as simple as reported speech and as complex as aesthetically sophisticated combinations of different speech genres, allusions, and hidden quotations. In a sufficiently developed verbal system, language serves as a context for itself. The process of cognitive decontextualization, therefore, cannot be accepted as a singular telos of verbal development, with facility in intralinguistic contextuality being an important goal as well.

Once the importance of contextually rich intralinguistic relations is acknowledged, the dichotomy of orality versus writing appears in a new light (Nystrand, 1986). Many "dialogical" features often associated with oral speech can be found in literary texts—and not as marginal elements, but as responsible for the superior quality of the texts in question. At the same time, the oral mode itself essentially depends on the mediation provided by written texts. One may conceive of two general types of oral exchanges: one based only on shared referentials pertaining to the extralinguistic world of things, and the other based on the knowledge of texts. In the second case, elements of texts known to interlocutors serve as mediators in communication and establish the necessary intersubjective connections. Interlocutors "participate" in the original texts, recognizing the "echo" of these texts in one another's speech. The shared texts provide that necessary base from which any further individual development of the topic of conversation can be started and to which the interlocutor can return, if misunderstood, as to a safe haven.

The alleged "autonomy" of scientific prose is also problematic (Cazden, 1989). The scientific paper is aimed at a very specific reader, a professional whose prior knowledge of the language involved is indispensable for the understanding of the paper. Scientific papers very rarely contain all required definitions, usually simply referring the reader to an appropriate body of literature. In a sense, the scientific paper represents almost zero autonomy, because it remains cryptic to any outsider. It should also be recognized that scientific statements about objective processes in nature are largely indifferent to the mode of expression: they can be made in the form of graphs, formulas, cartoons, oral speech, and so on. The verification of the "truth of correspondence" contained in these statements ultimately depends on the physical replication of the experimental procedures and not on conformity to the original text. It is, therefore, not only the "autonomous" but also the "textual" character of scientific papers that is suspect.

Still, Olson's (1989, p. 119) claim that "texts have a meaning independent of the authorial intention of their writers and the diverse interpretations of their readers" deserves closer scrutiny. One should, however, abandon the paradigm of the scientific paper and focus instead on religious, legal and poetic texts, which are also said to be "autonomous" or self-sufficient. An appropriate methodology here is that of a hermeneutic analysis (Gadamer, 1975; Mueller-Vollmer, 1985).

Autonomous texts are defined as those "which interpret themselves insofar as one needs no additional information about the occasion and the historical circumstances of their composition" (Gadamer, 1980, p. 86). Unlike the scientific paper, addressed to a narrow circle of specialists, the religious text addresses the entire community of believers, while poetic texts speak to an even wider and more indeterminate audience. "An 'autonomous text' is something which stands by itself, something to which one returns, a text which one may read again and again and which gains more richness when it becomes familiar" (Gadamer, 1980, p. 91).

It would be wrong to imagine that the problem of self-sufficiency is of purely academic interest for those engaged in religious exegesis or a study of poetics. The immediate relevance of the issue of self-sufficiency to contemporary social life is underscored by debates about the so-called original intent of the framers of the Constitution. The Constitution is a text that is relevant to situations that could not be foreseen by its authors, and thus its interpretation poses a clear-cut hermeneutic problem.

This peculiar ability of "autonomous texts" was noticed in the nineteenth century by Schleiermacher and was brought to our attention more recently by Gadamer: "The printed text should fix the original information <Kundgabe> in such a way that its sense is unequivocally understandable . . . To this extent, reading and understanding mean that information is led back to its original authenticity . . . However, this 'information' is *not what the speaker or writer originally said, but what he wanted to say indeed even more: what he would have wanted to say to me if I had been his original interlocutor*" (1986, p. 393, emphasis added).

Such understanding of the "autonomous text" implies that it must contain an interpretative "free space" that alone guarantees a meaningful rather than literal reading of the text, whose content cannot be negotiated with the author. Apparently Plato's dialogues and Shakespeare's tragedies contain just enough of such "free space" in order to be able to "speak" directly to the readers who are separated from the authors of these texts by time and space and who cannot re-create the authors' immediate extralinguistic experiences. The question thus arises: what allows some texts to function as self-sufficient and what cognitive consequences might this have for those whose psychological life is mediated by those texts?

In general theoretical terms the perpetual life of "autonomous texts" can be related to the phenomenon of "effective history" *(Wirkungsgeschichte)* (Gadamer (1975). The concept of "effective history" denotes—in simple terms—the presence of the past in the present. Our ability to understand the past essentially depends on our awareness of an overarching tradition which encompasses our point of view and that of the original text situated in the past. The original text, moreover, "lives" in history and lays its imprint on our language, our concepts, and our understanding of literature. The past text therefore is not only an object that we can approach in a detached manner, but also the source of our own verbal position. One may suggest that eminent autonomous texts, such as those of Plato and Shakespeare, are among the prime agents of the "effective history" permeating our verbal consciousness and on this basic level linking us to the past. Sometimes such influence is almost palpably obvious. For example, Russian language and literature since the early nineteenth century have one and the same source—the poetry of Alexander Pushkin. Not only a great poet, Pushkin was the true reformer of the national literary language and consequently everyday speech as well. Because his poetry became the norm of the national language, contemporary Russians immediately recognize his verses as "natural."

The process of "effective history" can be more closely defined through the notion of intertextuality. Intertextuality denotes, in a general sense, the transposition of one or several sign systems into another, and more specifically the presence of antecedent texts in consequent texts. Intertextuality thus provides a concrete linguistic mechanism for the presence of eminent autonomous texts in the verbal consciousness of people of later epochs. The phenomenon of intertextuality alerts us to at least the double nature of the word: the word is a signifier in respect to some extralinguistic signified, but it is also a signifier in a "response" to the antecedent signifier. "Any text is constructed as a mosaic of quotations; any text is the absorption and transformation of another. The notion of intertextuality replaces that of intersubjectivity, and poetic language is read as at least double" (Kristeva, 1986, p. 37).

Although I am not sure that Kristeva's "replacement" of intersubjectivity by intertextuality is not an exercise in deliberate theoretical extremism, it must be admitted that intersubjectivity often realizes itself in intertextuality. For psychology this has far-reaching consequences, because it points to the ambivalence of language as an individual/collective tool of thought and expression. Any act of verbal self-expression, for example, has an overtone in the form of intentional or unwitting "references" to preceding "texts." Moreover, these "texts" are present as an invisible "third" when any two people are engaged in oral or written conversation. Apart from certain special cases, the preceding texts are present not as actual fragments or allusions but, rather, as semantic archetypes (for example, a root metaphor like "man-as-a-machine" or "life-as-a-road").

I suggest that the special importance of the eminent "autonomous texts" is determined by their status as powerful sources of such archetypes. Their eminence is based on the ability to cast some fundamental problem in a form that cannot be supplanted. These archetypes become a part of our everyday speech and we return to them, for the most part unconsciously, when we attempt to produce novel texts.

Thus the second implication of cultural psychology for education is that not only decontextualized thinking but intertextually rich discourse should become a criterion of cognitive maturity. To achieve this maturity students should be made aware of the connection between classical "autonomous texts" and the form of verbal reasoning they are using.

## Literary Form as Consciousness

The moment one accepts that literature is an important mediator which shapes human cognitive processes, one cannot be satisfied any longer with such gross dichotomies as "writing versus orality" or "literate mind versus preliterate mind." What is needed is a much more detailed study of the historically changing role of literature as a higher-order psychological tool (Kozulin, 1993).

As a first step in this direction I will explore the distinction between the cognitive role of "classical" literature of the nineteenth century and the "modernist" literature of the twentieth. The ongoing theoretical debates about the phenomenon of "modernity" and "postmodernity" (Adorno, 1984; Habermas, 1987) have produced convincing evidence that the position of high culture in Western society changed dramatically in the course of the nineteenth century. The symptoms of this change have been described in different terms, but in essence all of them point to the "secession" of high culture from the organic whole of social life. In the beginning of the nineteenth century, high culture was still tied by thousands of strings to the everyday life of the upper classes. Belonging to the upper class almost automatically presupposed a certain type of education and an acquaintance with a certain class of literary texts. In a sense it was impossible for an individual to have a "life in culture" separate from social existence; high culture was inseparable from the individual's social position and social habits. Of course there were individuals for whom the production and consumption of high culture was of much greater importance than for others. But even their preoccupation with culture was rarely perceived as an existence in a separate realm. Within literature itself, its intertextual aspect was still firmly entangled with the social aspect. Intertextuality, though always present, was not yet deliberately emphasized. High culture did not put a wall between itself and the world of everyday experience, and did not focus on the task of creating a separate literary universe. Nineteenth-century literature could still speak directly about social reality (thus its "realism"), because its authors and readers shared this reality and its reflections in the universals of high culture in their individual experiences.

The breakdown of traditional social order, which was already apparent in the 1860s (Gaunt, 1967) but became accepted as irreversible only in the 1930s, produced, among other things, the radical displacement of high culture from its "natural" base in the social universe of the upper classes. This breakdown of the traditional links between high culture and the social order put culture in a new position. It was impossible any longer to take for granted the shared cultural and social horizon of the author and his readers. It is not surprising that such a denaturalization of high culture's existence prompted it to put forward fundamental questions about its own self-determination and self-definition. The problem was no longer how to write or study poetry, but what was poetry (Lemon and Reis, 1965). At the same time, the displacement of high culture from its natural social context created a precondition for the self-conscious "life in culture."

"Life in culture" appeared as both an aesthetic approach and a social phenomenon. As a social and existential position, "life in culture" became a spiritual (and physical) survival technique of members of the intelligentsia persecuted by Stalinist and other totalitarian regimes. In this respect the evolution in the views of the poet Osip Mandelstam is quite revealing. In his early postrevolutionary essays Mandelstam expressed near exultation at the idea of a complete breakdown of the old social order, which among other things allegedly maintained false relationships between social and cultural horizons. In the new, postrevolutionary reality, culture, according to Mandelstam, was completely free—unsupported by the social order, but also not bound by it. Living in culture seemed very exciting, at least for the poet. Several years later, "life in culture" acquired a new meaning for Mandelstam, who was persecuted and ultimately killed by Stalin's regime. New relationships, and rather nightmarish ones, were established between the new social order and what remained of high culture. For those who were not ready to enter into these new relationships, the only choice was to cultivate "life in culture" as the last form of personal defense (Mandelstam, 1979).

As an aesthetic position, "life in culture" realizes itself in a radical intertextuality that presents culture as a chain of signifiers. Probably the best-known author whose writings elevate conscious intertextuality to the level of the universal cultural attitude is Jorge Luis Borges. A contemporary critic observed: "In his aesthetic elaboration Borges moves in a world of quotations . . . His stories are allusions to other stories, his characters are allusions to other characters, and their lives are allusions to other lives" (Christ, 1969, pp. 34–35).

Borges pushed to its limit the literary device of allusion by creating, for example, the pseudoessay "Pierre Menard the Author of Don Quixote" in which a fictitious author of a fictitious book allegedly rewrites Cervantes's novel, arriving at the same text as that of Cervantes but, predictably, with a different meaning (Borges, 1962). Borges thus achieved two goals. First, he asserted the primacy of text in respect to life, with life becoming an allusion to the text. The primacy of text, long recognized as a major "thesis" of modernist culture, reached its total domination in Borges's writings where, in a sense, there is no other action than the literary one. Second, Borges collapsed the time, or more precisely the linear time, of unified sociocultural history. The collapse of time allowed him to operate with different cultural epochs as coexistent, copresent. This constitutes the radical shift of literature's method toward that of philology. One would find nothing strange in the copresence, for example, of Humboldt's and Heidegger's views on language on one page of a philological text; at the same time a literary description of an "actual" dialogue between Humboldt and Heidegger regarding language would be considered a modernist trick. The collapse of time is essential for the implementation of a consciously intertextual cultural position, because it "liberates" the culture from its fixed attachments to a specific social and physical reality. In Borges's universe of collapsed time the culture becomes truly a chain of signifiers that have a life of their own.

While Borges laid bare the device of deliberate intertextuality, it was another modern author, Mikhail Bulgakov (1967), who took a further step and painted a picture of social reality as seen through the lens of conscious intertextuality. Bulgakov's novel *The Master and Margarita* is chosen here not only because it expresses a very innovative relationship between the text and social reality, but also because of the enormous influence this novel has on the mentality of Russian readers. Written in the 1930s by an author who was both shunned and haunted by Stalin's regime, the novel was published for the first time only in the 1960s and immediately became one of the most cherished and discussed works of Russian literature (Proffer, 1984). Its influence on the public mentality was so strong that certain phrases from the book were quickly adopted as new proverbs.

The circumstances under which the novel was written in the 1930s have a direct bearing on the problem of "life in culture" as a social phenomenon. Bulgakov was quite aware of the complete rupture between the social order he had to live under and the cultural tradition he belonged to. The only authentic state of being for the author in such circumstances is being in the realm of culture rejected by society. Bulgakov's novel is populated by characters who are impossible in the Stalinist social reality: an outcast author (the Master), Mephistopheles (Voland), Jesus (Yehoshua Ha-Nozri). These characters are archetypical figures of European high culture, excluded from the official sociocultural realm of the Stalinist state.

Bulgakov employs many of the devices already mentioned here in conjunction with Borges's work. There is a collapse of time and historical reality in Bulgakov's novel, with Mephistopheles, Pontius Pilate, and the Soviet apparatchiks all present in the Moscow of the 1920s. There is also a strong assertion of the primacy of text, from the novel's key phrase, "Manuscripts do not burn," to the fact that events in Moscow have a direct relation to the events of Passion Week in Jerusalem as they are narrated in the novel within a novel allegedly written by the Master. Bulgakov, however, did not limit himself to the creation of a separate literary reality into which he and his readers could escape from a hostile social environment. Bulgakov took a truly radical step: in his novel the perspective of rejected culture becomes a springboard for a comprehensive satirical critique of the official sociocultural reality. Bulgakov's is not the usual literary-social critique. Unlike his nineteenth-century predecessors, he did not pit one set of social ideals against the other while remaining on the plane of a commonly shared sociocultural reality. Society in Bulgakov's novel is denied the status of a given reality; it becomes transposed onto a plane of strictly cultural evaluation where its grotesque essence is revealed in a masterly way. Bulgakov's is a formal critique in the sense that it is not a critique of social content from the position of shared cultural form, but a radical "estrangement" of the critic's cultural position itself.

The dual nature of the literary word, as a "sign for a thing" and as a "sign for a sign," is fully employed in Bulgakov's novel. Each dialogue and each episode can be read both in the plane of reference to apparent social and historical events, and in the plane of rich allusions to cultural texts unrelated to these events. As a result a new literary reality is created that has as one of its focuses Jerusalem during Passion Week, where selected pieces from Pushkin and Chekhov are quoted as sacred commandments, and as another Moscow of the 1920s, where, with reference to Dostoyevsky, a *Roman aktuell* about events in Jerusalem is written (Kaganskaja and Bar-Sella, 1984).

A modernist literary device thus becomes an extremely potent aesthetic weapon in the liberation of the reader's consciousness. This consciousness no longer accepts the official sociocultural horizon as the only real one. For the new consciousness generated by Bulgakov's novel, this official horizon becomes simply irrelevant. Taking into account the influence of Bulgakov's work, which transcended the literary sphere and reached for the consciousness of Russian readers, one may wonder whether this is not a revealing case of the role of literature as a psychological tool. What we have here is a higher-order "psychological tool"— the novel—which with its formal structure and historically specific manner succeeded in altering the very method of people's comprehension of their social existence.

The full social power of literature as a psychological tool revealed itself with unusual force in the case of *The Satanic Verses* (1989) by Salman Rushdie. This novel drew much public attention because of the death warrant issued against its author by Iranian fundamentalists. *The Satanic Verses,* however, is far from being an ordinary political satire. Like Bulgakov, Rushdie offers a radically "estranged" view of both East and West, of both politics and religion. Milan Kundera, an expatriate Czech writer and essayist, perceives Rushdie's as a cause célèbre not of political oppression, but of culture's power. "Rushdie did not blaspheme. He did not attack Islam. He wrote a novel. But that, for the theocratic mind is worse than an attack: if a religion is attacked (by a polemic, a blasphemy, a heresy), the guardians of the temple can easily defend it on their own ground, with their own language; but the novel is a different planet for them; a different universe based on a different ontology; an *infernum* where the unique truth is powerless and where satanic ambiguity turns every certainty into enigma" (Kundera 1995, p. 26).

In his novel Rushdie uses many of the literary devices already mentioned. Three apparently unrelated story lines coexist: the lives of

Gibreel Farishta and Saladin Chamcha, two present-day Indians who divide their time between Bombay and London; the Koranic story dealing with the origin of Islam; and a story of a group of villagers who make a pilgrimage across the sea, believing they can cross it on foot. The characters' behavior cannot, however, be deduced from their own story lines. For example, Gibreel Farishta cannot be understood without reference to the Archangel Gabriel. The characters live multiple lives, one connected to "their story" but others connected to various other texts—some explicitly hinted at, some more implicit. One can even find some scenes that refer to *The Master and Margarita*.

Rushdie's satire is universal; it leaves nothing intact, neither West not East, neither fanatic religiosity nor modern pop culture. The reader is educated to be both reflective and relativistic. There is no place here for straightforward approval or indignation. If the reader is about to be offended by the manner in which the Koranic story is presented, he or she is "reminded" that this story is a dream of Gibreel Farishta, a dream that he then develops into a cheap and unsuccessful movie. Kundera (1995, p. 26) comments that "the story is doubly relativized."

If taken as empirically given, different linguistic, social, and historical positions can hardly be comprehended and reconciled. But when they become different textual "voices" in one aesthetically accomplished whole their complementarity becomes accessible. The modern novel of the kind created by Bulgakov and Rushdie serves as a tool that develops in its reader a cognitive capacity for such a multidimensional comprehension.

Thus the third implication of cultural psychology for education is that higher-order "psychological tools" such as a specific literary approach permeating the whole of a literary work may serve as potent instruments for changing the consciousness of the student reader. To fulfill this role, this approach should be identified and made available in its "instrumental" capacity to students.

## Education and Modernity

The phenomenon of modernity has a number of social aspects such as industrialization, rationalization, the breakdown of traditional order, alienation, and so on. Here I am concerned with just one of modernity's characteristic features: its sociocultural pluralism. Sociocultural pluralism results from the insertion of previously self-contained and self-sufficient groups into one all-embracing sociocultural system. Bakhtin (1973) stated: "Those worlds and those planes—social, cultural and ideological—which collide in Dostoyevsky's work were in the past self-sufficient, organically self-enclosed, consolidated, and had inner significance as separate units. Capitalism destroyed the isolation of these worlds and broke down the seclusion and inner ideological self-sufficiency of those social spheres . . . Their blind co-existence, and their blissful and self-assured state of mutual ideological ignorance came to an end; their mutual contradictoriness and, at the same time, their mutual connectedness were exposed with utmost clarity" (p. 15).

For education, sociocultural pluralism and the concomitant democratization of schooling poses a serious problem. In the premodern period, education was based on a certain universal model of human experience that usually had religious or mythological foundations. Such a model served as a natural presupposition for both teachers and students. Teachers represented an unambiguous cultural tradition associated with this model, and their task was to transmit and articulate it to the student. Thus teachers, who possessed an undeniable authoritative voice, were supposed to find didactic means for the transmission of this unambiguous tradition. Under new, modern conditions it became incumbent on teachers to establish and defend the nonarbitrary character of the chosen cultural position. Because teachers cannot rely on the shared cultural horizon between themselves and their students, they are forced to rediscover this tradition anew.

Traditional education was essentially retrospective. The universal model and the cultural tradition were givens, and the task of a student was to absorb this tradition and the intellectual tools associated with it. Thus a student was taught to deal with problems that reproduced past cultural patterns. Under the dynamic conditions of modernity the necessity for prospective, rather than retrospective, education became obvious (Silvestrov, 1989). Prospective education implies that students should be capable of approaching problems that do not yet exist at the moment of his or her learning. To achieve this capability, the student should be oriented toward productive, rather than reproductive, knowledge. Knowledge should thus appear not in the form of results and solutions but rather as a process of authoring.

Here the model provided by the humanities has certain advantages over that of science. The progressivist interpretation of science presents earlier theories either as fallacies or as approximations to modern ones. In this context, the process of authoring is obscured by the final result. Something new always appears better than something old. The humanities suggest an alternative model, because it is impossible to say that Tolstoy is better than Shakespeare or that Hegel is better than Plato. The humanities not only focus our attention on the process of authoring but also provide a paradigm for a genuine dialogue of cultures (Bibler, 1989). In the modern mind, Plato, Hegel, Shakespeare, and Tolstoy represent cultural traditions which are irreducible to one another, but which at the same time are mutually complementary as different attempts at solving the same set of fundamental problems.

A study of the classical autonomous texts returns the student to the beginnings of the world's fundamental artistic and scientific problems. These problems appear, therefore, as problems rather than as solutions. Such a "return to the beginning" is characteristic for any genuine authoring, both humanistic and scientific. In this sense, each great poet is writing poetry anew, each great philosopher wrestles with the fundamental enigma of human consciousness, and each great scientist returns to the problem of causality in nature. The return to the beginning, necessitated by the situation of modernity, provides an opportunity for prospective education, based on the model of authoring rather than on reproduction. Historically, the authoring model not only is derived from the humanities but is used as an educational guideline in teaching the humanities. This guideline, however, can be as readily applied to the work of Newton and Einstein as it has been to that of Plato and Tolstoy.

Thus the last implication for education is that the return to the beginning and the dialogical type of learning characteristic of the humanities could be extended to teaching science. Through this, the intertextual and conceptual decontextualized types of cognition can be successfully combined.

## Conclusion

In this chapter we have explored the possibilities of a literary model for psychology. Literature may serve both as a prototype of the most advanced form of human psychological life and as a specific "psychological tool" mediating human experiences.

The "life as authoring" approach based on the work of Bakhtin helps us to grasp the constructive nature of the self. The self cannot be reduced to its here-and-now characteristics but can be reconstructed through its synchronous and diachronous projections. The relationships between the author and his or her characters, particularly in such genres as autobiography, provide important cues on how such "construction" is achieved.

The notion of literature as a psychological tool leads us beyond the dichotomy of orality versus writing and poses the question of the historically changing role of literary devices as internalized forms of verbal consciousness. Modernist literature supplies human cognition with devices that facilitate a radical critical approach to social reality.

Language, as it reveals itself in literary texts, helps us to correct a popular yet misleading view of cognitive development as dependent primarily on decontextualized mental operations. In a verbal system that is sufficiently developed, language serves as a context for itself. Thus a facility with intertextual relationships is an important aspect of the development of verbal consciousness.

The modern situation characterized by sociocultural pluralism not only poses serious problems for education but forces it to see new opportunities. One of them is a "return to the beginning" associated with prospective education. This education is oriented toward a re-creation of fundamental problems rather than learning existent solutions. Such a re-creation is possible within the authoring model developed in the humanities. This model, however, can also be used in teaching science.

# 7 ✒

# The Challenges of Prospective Education

Traditional education responded to society's goal of transmitting an unambiguous cultural tradition from generation to generation, and in this respect was for the most part retrospective. The model of the world and cultural tradition were givens, and the task of a student was to absorb this tradition and the intellectual tools associated with it. Students were thus taught to deal with problems that reproduced the cultural patterns of the past. Under the dynamic conditions of modernity, the necessity for prospective, rather than retrospective, education becomes obvious. Prospective education implies that students should be capable of approaching problems that do not yet exist. To gain this ability, students should be oriented toward productive rather than reproductive knowledge. Thus the body of knowledge should appear not in the form of results and solutions but as a creative process, the process of "authoring." The student should be involved in "co-authoring" the fundamental laws and principles of a given field. The focus of learning thus shifts from delivering information to the student to building the student's learning potential. The changing goals of education both reflect the objective shifts in the triangle of relationships among student, teacher, and material, and inform these shifts.

## Traditional Roles and Relationships

To understand changes occurring in the student–teacher–material triangle, let us first examine their traditional roles and relationships within the educational system.

*Learning material* as understood in the traditional system contained primarily information and operational rules. The composition of learning material took into consideration the information in a given field, such as history, geography, literature, or science, that society deemed necessary for a school graduate to acquire in order to become an educated individual. In addition to sheer information, students were also provided with rules that allowed them to perform certain operations, for example, to work with mathematical formulae or to check the correctness of spelling and syntactic constructions. The units of material were supposed to be transmitted to the student and stored in his or her memory together with attached operators allowing for the appropriate retrieval of necessary information and/or rules. Students' ability to comprehend material and approach it as a problem was taken for granted as a function of their natural cognitive maturity level.

The *teacher* in the traditional system had three roles, serving as a conduit of learning material to the student, evaluating students' progress and achievements, and serving as a model of the accomplished educated individual. The first two of these functions were largely constrained by the content of the curriculum and the achievement requirements set up by educational authorities. The third function allowed a greater latitude for the teacher, but depended almost entirely on his or her own individual initiative. In principle, the teacher could reduce his or her role as an expert learner to the exemplary reproduction of rules and information already contained in the learning material.

The *child* in the traditional system was perceived primarily as a recipient of learning material delivered to him or her by the teacher (Strauss, 1993). The task of the child was to absorb this material, learn the rules, and be able to display both material and rules upon request. Children were expected to possess certain normative psychological characteristics, such as memory and attention capacities, allowing them to participate in a regular school, learning at a certain grade level. If children failed to manifest these capacities, they were pronounced intellectually unfit for regular education and shifted to the special education track.

## New Roles and Relationships

Let us now explore how this traditional learning system and the relationships inherent in it have changed under the influence of the social and educational requirements characteristic of a modern society (Burden, 1994).

## Education and Development

The child's position vis-à-vis the process of school learning has been changed in the direction of acknowledging that school learning contributes not only to the child's education but to the child's development. Vygotsky's sociocultural theory has contributed significantly to this change in our understanding of the relationships between development and education. If in the traditional system the child's development was perceived as a natural maturational process, necessary for, but mostly unaffected by, education, in the modern system the child's development is perceived as dependent on sociocultural forces embodied in formal and informal education. Thus the goal of education is not only to educate in the narrow sense of this term, but also to develop the child. The child's achievements, therefore, should be evaluated not only in terms of the acquisition of material but also in terms of the development of general and specific cognitive strategies (Presseisen, 1987). These strategies, in turn, are evaluated both in terms of their immediate learning benefits and as a basis for further development. As a result of this shift new relationships are established between psychologists and educators. Psychological assessment becomes oriented toward educational intervention, while the educational process is supposed to bring about changes in the child's cognitive functions (Lidz, 1987a).

## The Child's Activity

Far from being a passive recipient of information and rules, the child in the modern system is recognized as an active learner who explores, selects, and transforms learning material. The modern system offers two major alternatives in approaching the issue of the child's activity. One of them is connected to Piagetian theory and assumes that what children need is a stimulating problem-solving environment within which they can develop and practice their mental schemas (Duckworth, 1978). Within the limits of their stage of cognitive development children are perceived as independent learners whose initiative, curiosity, and ability to discover are the major factors of the educational process. The second alternative can be linked to Vygotsky's theory. It claims that the child as an independent learner is an outcome rather than a starting point of the educational process (Kozulin, 1994). Different forms of children's activity, which may be practical, playful, interpersonal, and so on, should be organized and transformed in order to produce genuine learning activity in the child. Creating conditions generative of such learning activity is one of the primary tasks of school vis-à-vis the child. This position is "constructivist" in the sense that it takes into account the child's spontaneously formed concepts and encourages the child's co-authoring of knowledge. The child, however, cannot be left to his or her premises in this constructive activity. This activity should be guided along the lines of disciplinary knowledge and concept formation.

## Diversity of the Learners' Population

The diversity of the modern student population dictates new approaches. Age-related differences in the cognitive functioning of the child no longer constitute the major factor determining the nomenclature of didactic approaches. In the modern system children differ in their formal and informal educational backgrounds, language experience (bi- and multilingualism), presence of specific learning difficulties, and so on. All these factors should be taken into account in designing a comprehensive classroom strategy. It is impossible simply to segregate all the "unsuitable" students into separate classes. The problem of teaching a heterogeneous class thus comes to the fore.

## Learning Materials

The major transformation undergone by learning materials in the modern system reflects the new relationships between learning activities and learning material. As long as learning activities were limited to teachers lecturing and students responding to oral or written questions, learning materials could be limited to content-subject narratives and collections of standard math and science problems. With the advance of education based on the foundation of learning activities, the role of learning materials has been changed. On the one hand, new learning materials are supposed to support learning activities. The workbook for a nature class, for example, is organized in such a way as to support observational, experimentation, and discussion activities carried out in the class. On the other hand, learning materials themselves, including text- and workbooks, problem sheets, experiment kits, and computer programs, are designed with the internal goal of eliciting a specific learning activity. This changing role of learning materials from that of carriers of information to that of generators of activity reflects a more general shift from an emphasis on the product of learning (for example, correct spelling, automatization of mathematical operations, correct recollection of data) to an emphasis on the process of learning (reading for meaning, the far-transfer of mathematical principles, the ability to identify and define the task in unfamiliar material, and so on). The new role of learning materials also reflects a growing recognition of the importance of cognitive development through education. Learning material is now as much responsible for the development of thinking skills as it used to be responsible for providing content knowledge.

## Teachers

In the modern educational system the teacher receives both more freedom and more responsibility in selecting learning materials and activities. Teachers are becoming more and more involved in the design and testing of learning materials and didactic approaches. This new freedom and new responsibility demand from the teacher a much greater flexibility and creativity in selecting appropriate educational genres. Lectures, student recitations, and standardized written tests—these typical genres of traditional education constitute only a fraction of the interactive forms available to the contemporary teacher. Different activities ranging from scientific demonstration experiments to simulated civic forums and small group computer-supported learning sessions are all within the teacher's reach, although all require his or her planning and control. Modern-day teachers are called upon to work in a heterogeneous classroom populated by children with radically different educational, cultural, and linguistic backgrounds. This means that teachers can no longer attune their teaching to the "average" student, but are forced to develop a whole set of educational scripts deployed simultaneously to respond to the differing needs of students. Moreover, as the teacher's cultural horizon often fails to coincide with that of his or her students, the nonarbitrary character of many "obvious" cultural standards should be demonstrated and defended by the teacher. All of this renders teachers' work much more creative, but also more demanding.

## The Sociocultural Approach

The sociocultural approach based on Vygotsky's theory (1978, 1986, 1994) and its later elaborations (Wertsch, 1985b; Moll, 1990; Forman, Minick, and Addison Stone, 1993) both promoted some of the changes outlined above and was called on to provide tools for coping with them.

### *Human Agency as Nonindividualistic*

One of Vygotsky's major theoretical contributions was his challenge to the prevailing view on human agency as a property of the individual. He perceived human agency as nonindividualistic in two respects: first, it is often a property of dyads and other small groups, and second, the cultural nature of human psychological tools "extends" human agency beyond that of a given individual (Wertsch, Tulviste, and Hagstrom, 1993). Such a nonindividualistic interpretation of human agency has immediate consequences for psychological and educational theory. The border between the "natural" and the "cultural" should be redrawn. What seemed to be a natural function belonging to an individual (for example, speech) appears in this new perspective as an internalized outcome of sociocultural interactions. One and the same function—for example, memory or attention—appears in two radically different forms if perceived as an individual's property, on the one hand, and as a function of symbolic processes that became appropriated by the individual from his or her culture and that in this sense is superindividual, on the other. Thus the emphasis in educational and school psychology is shifting from the identification of students' individual abilities and propensities toward socially constructed activities aimed at the development of learning potential and higher psychological functions of the student.

## Psychological Tools

According to Vygotsky (1978, 1986, 1994), the major distinctive feature of human learning and psychological development lies in the involvement of symbolic psychological tools in this process. Signs, writing, numerical systems, formulae, graphs, and other symbolic devices radically change the process of learning, allowing students to organize and regulate their own cognitive processes with the help of these cultural tools. One of the essential characteristics of learning based on psychological tools is its ability to use *models,* that is, schematized and generalized representations of objects, processes, and their relationships. Moreover, students' own thinking and problem-solving activity can be represented as a model with the help of psychological tools, thus becoming an object of the students' conscious deliberation, planning, and decision making.

Psychological tools are introduced into the learning process in two different contexts. One of them is the context of content learning, where psychological tools provide the necessary cognitive component essential for the comprehension of material and the development of thinking associated with this material. The other context is that of special cognitive education programs, the main goal of which is to make psychological tools available for students who for a variety of reasons may lack them.

One may distinguish two groups of psychological tools. The more basic psychological tools, including signs, graphic-symbolic devices, and writing and numerical systems, are essential for the acquisition of the most general of formal learning skills required at school. These tools are relatively content free in a sense that their mastery is needed in all content areas and their learning can be organized as an independent cognitive education activity. Higher-order psychological tools are more closely related to the relevant fields of knowledge. At this higher level psychological tools often acquire a form of domain-specific concepts and organizing devices, thus bridging the gap between the cognitive and content aspects of learning. Both the sciences and the humanities have their own systems of higher-order symbolic tools characteristic of specific areas of knowledge. One may thus speak about different disciplinary languages in a formal rather than metaphorical sense. Mathematics, physics, philosophy, literary criticism, and other fields have their own languages, that is, systems of representing, organizing, and operating symbolic devices. These devices are not arbitrary but reflect objective sociocultural practices that lead to the formation of a given field of knowledge.

The task of modern education is first and foremost to teach students these different languages. Once such a disciplinary literacy is acquired it is much easier for students to face the task of prospective and continuing learning, which requires the mastery of material unknown at the time of their initial training.

## Zone of Proximal Development

The notion of the zone of proximal development points to the fact that students' learning occurs not only on the basis of fully established psychological functions but also using functions that are not yet fully formed (Vygotsky, 1978, 1986; see also Van der Veer and Valsiner, 1993). This is possible because learning occurs not in isolation but in collaboration between a student and an adult or more competent peers. ZPD is operationalized as the distance between the student's level of independent problem solving and the level of his or her problem solving when it is guided or facilitated by the other more competent individual. The notion of ZPD has significant consequences for both learning assessment and teaching practices. Static tests that evaluate the manifest level of the student's functioning become challenged by learning potential tests based on the notion of ZPD (Lidz, 1995). In teaching, the notion of ZPD stimulates the development of reciprocal, guided, and mediated learning programs (Forman, Minick, and Addison Stone, 1993). These programs focus on the learning that takes place in "collaborative space" between the student and the teacher. They both utilize the student's existent ZPD and further enhance it.

## Collaborative Learning

The issue of collaborative learning is deeply embedded in Vygotskian theory and practice, starting with the famous statement that interpsychological ("between people") processes become intrapsychological ("within a person") processes (Vygotsky, 1978). Vygotsky's followers (Elkonin, 1971; Rubtsov, 1991) developed this thesis in two directions. First, in the context of Elkonin's (1971) theory of age-specific leading activities, it was postulated that the activity of interpersonal communication constitutes a predominant activity during late adolescence. Learning based on collaborative activity thus has a greater chance of success at this age, because instead of fighting the students' tendency to talk to one another during the lesson, it uses this tendency for educational goals. Second, the issue of collaborative learning was linked to the notions of learning activity and psychological tools (Rubtsov, 1991). Instead of simply studying the influence of a group situation on individual problem solving as is done by neo-Piagetians (Doise and Mugny, 1984), neo-Vygotskians suggested studying learning activity as deliberately constructed on the basis of collaborative learning.

An important component of such a learning activity is the symbolic psychological tools (schemas, maps, and charts) representing the distribution of activities among participating students. As a result the cooperative learning situation encompasses a number of elements:

1. The task, which requires both specific operations with objects and a change in the student's own method of action.
2. A group of students who have problem-solving operations and actions distributed among them. The students communicate with one another, exchange their methods of action, and explain their actions to one another.
3. Graphic models representing the relationships between operations with objects and collectively distributed methods of action.

In a number of studies reported by Rubtsov (1991), it was shown that younger students benefited from collaborative learning activities while solving problems that required class inclusion. Older students demonstrated greater mastery of physical problem solving (topic: magnetic field) when it included collaborative activity mediated by graphic models that represented the participants' actions. The criterion of mastery was the formation of the theoretical, rather than the empirical, notion of the magnetic field, which allowed the solution of the whole range of different problems.

## Conclusion

This chapter summarizes some of the challenges brought about by the changes occurring in modern education in the triangle of relationships among students, teachers, and learning materials. Vygotskian and neo-Vygotskian theory offers a number of responses to these challenges. One of the pivotal elements of the Vygotskian approach is the perception of the educational process as contributing primarily to the cognitive development of the student. Specially designed learning activities can empower a student to become a competent and ultimately independent learner. Learning activities include symbolic psychological tools and collaborative learning procedures as two of their major constitutive elements. It is essential that these activities and tools be mediated by a human intermediary. The applications mentioned earlier represent only samples of learning activities that can be constructed on the basis of sociocultural theory. The task of psychology and education is to fully realize the applied potential inherent in this theory.

# References

Adams, H., and Wallace, B. 1993. The "Thinking Activity in a Social Context" (TASC) Project. In H. Adams and B. Wallace, eds., *Worldwide Perspectives on Gifted Disadvantaged*, pp. 44–66. Bicester, UK: A B Academic Publishers.

Adorno, T. W. 1984. *Aesthetic Theory*. London: Routledge & Kegan Paul.

Asnin, V. [1941] 1980. The Development of Visual-Operational Thinking in Children. *Soviet Psychology*, 18(2): 23–26.

August-Rothman, P., and Zinn, B. 1986. Application of IE Principles to a Mathematics Course for Young Ethiopian Adults. Project Summary. Student Counseling Services. Hebrew University, Jerusalem.

Bakhtin, M. 1973. *Dostoevsky's Poetics*. Ann Arbor, Mich.: Ardis.

——— 1986. *Speech Genres and Other Late Essays*. Austin: University of Texas Press.

——— 1990. *Art and Answerability*. Austin: University of Texas Press.

Ballmer, T. 1981. A Typology of Native Speakers. In F. Coulmans ed., *A Festschrift for Native Speakers*, pp. 51–67. The Hague: Mouton.

Barthes, R. 1982. *Barthes' Reader*. New York: Hill & Wang.

Ben-Hur, M., ed. 1994. *On Feuerstein's Instrumental Enrichment*. Palatine, Ill.: IRI/Skylight.

Berk, L., and Garvin, R. 1984. Development of Private Speech among Low-Income Appalachian Children. *Developmental Psychology*, 20(2): 271–286.

Beyer, B. 1991. *Teaching Thinking Skills: A Handbook for Secondary School Teachers*. Boston: Allyn & Bacon.

Bibler, V. 1989. On the Philosophical Logic of Paradox. *Soviet Studies in Philosophy*, 28: 3–15.

Blumer, H. 1969. *Symbolic Interactionism*. Englewood Cliffs, N.J.: Prentice Hall.

Borges, J. L. 1962. *Labyrinths*. New York: New Directions.

Brainerd, C. 1978. *Piaget's Theory of Intelligence*. Englewood Cliffs, N.J.: Prentice Hall.

Bransford, J., Arbitman-Smith, R., Stein, B., and Vye, N. 1985. Improving Thinking and Learning Skills: An Analysis of Three Approaches. In J. Segal, S. Chapman, and R. Glaser, eds., *Thinking and Learning Skills: Relating Instruction to Research*, pp. 133–208. Hillsdale, N.J.: Lawrence Erlbaum Associates.

Bronfenbrenner, U. 1979. *The Ecology of Human Development*. Cambridge, Mass.: Harvard University Press.

Bronson, G. W. 1968. The Development of Fear in Man and Other Animals. *Child Development*, 39: 409–430.

Brown, A., and Ferrara, R. 1985. Diagnosing Zones of Proximal Development. In J. Wertsch, ed., *Culture, Communication, and Cognition.* New York: Cambridge University Press.

Bruner, J. 1986. *Actual Minds, Possible Worlds.* Cambridge, Mass.: Harvard University Press.

———— 1987. Life as Narrative. *Social Research,* 54: 11–32.

Bugrimenko, E., and Elkonin, B. D. 1994. Znakovoe Oposredstvovanie v Processah Formirovaniia i Razvitiia (Sign Mediation in the Processes of Formation and Development). *Vestnik Moskovskogo Universiteta: Psikhologiia,* 4: 27–35.

Bulgakov, M. 1967. *The Master and Margarita.* Trans. Mirra Ginsburg. New York: Grove Press.

Burden, R. 1994. Trends and Developments in Educational Psychology. *School Psychology International,* 15(4): 293–347.

Campione, J., and Brown, A. 1987. Linking Dynamic Assessment with School Achievement. In C. Lidz, ed., *Dynamic Assessment,* pp. 82–115. New York: Guilford Press.

Carey, S. 1985. *Conceptual Change in Childhood.* Cambridge, Mass.: MIT Press.

Cazden, C. 1989. The Myth of Autonomous Text. In D. M. Topping, D. C. Crowell, and V. N. Kobayashi, eds., *Thinking across Cultures.* Hillsdale, N.J.: Lawrence Erlbaum.

Christ, R. 1969. *The Narrow Act: Borges's Art of Allusion.* New York: New York University Press.

Claparede, E. 1959. Preface. In J. Piaget, *The Thought and Language of the Child.* London: Routledge & Kegan Paul.

Clark, K., and Holquist, M. 1984. *Mikhail Bakhtin.* Cambridge, Mass.: Harvard University Press.

Cole, M. 1980. The Kharkov School of Developmental Psychology. *Soviet Psychology,* 18(2): 3–8.

———— 1990. Cognitive Development and Formal Schooling. In L. Moll, ed., *Vygotsky and Education,* pp. 89–110. New York: Cambridge University Press.

Cole, M., Gay, J., Glick, J., and Sharp, D. 1971. *The Cultural Contexts of Learning and Thinking.* New York: Basic Books.

Cole, M., and Scribner, S. 1974. *Culture and Thought.* New York: Wiley.

Collingnon Filipek, F. 1994. From "Paj ntaub" to Paragraphs: Perspectives on Hmong Processes of Composing. In V. John-Steiner, C. Panofsky, and L. Smith, eds., *Sociocultural Approaches to Language and Literacy,* pp. 331–346. New York: Cambridge University Press.

Costa, A. 1985. *Developing Minds: A Resource Book for Teaching Thinking.* Alexandria, Va.: Association for Supervision and Curriculum Development.

Cromer, R. 1991. *Language and Thought in Normal and Handicapped Children.* Cambridge, Mass.: Basil Blackwell.

Cummins, J. 1989. Institutionalized Racism and the Assessment of Minority Children. In R. Samuda, S. Kong, J. Cummins, J. Pascual-Leone, and J. Lewis, eds., *Assessment and Placement of Minority Students*, pp. 95–107. Toronto: Hogrefe.

Davydov, V. 1988a. The Concept of Theoretical Generalization. *Studies in Soviet Thought*, 36: 169–202.

———— 1988b. Problems of Developmental Teaching, parts I–III. *Soviet Education*, 30: 8–10.

Davydov, V., and Radzikhovsky, L. 1985. Vygotsky's Theory and the Activity-Oriented Approach. In J. Wertsch, ed., *Culture, Communication, and Cognition*, pp. 35–65. New York: Cambridge University Press.

Diaz, R., and Berk, L., eds. 1992. *Private Speech: From Social Interaction to Self-Regulation*. Hillsdale, N.J.: Lawrence Erlbaum Associates.

Dixon-Krauss, L., ed. 1996. *Vygotsky in the Classroom*. London: Longman.

Doise, W., and Mugny, G. 1984. *The Social Development of the Intellect*. Oxford: Pergamon Press.

Duckworth, E. 1987. *The Having of Wonderful Ideas and Other Essays on Teaching and Learning*. New York: Teachers College Press.

Egan, K. 1997. *The Educated Mind*. Chicago: Chicago University Press.

Ellenberger, H. 1970. *The Discovery of the Unconscious*. New York: Basic Books.

Elkonin, D. 1971. Toward the Problem of Stages in the Mental Development of the Child. *Soviet Psychology*, 10: 538–653.

Erikson, E. 1963. *Childhood and Society*. New York: Norton.

Feuerstein, R. 1990. The Theory of Structural Cognitive Modifiability. In B. Presseisen, ed., *Learning and Thinking Styles: Classroom Interaction*, pp. 68–134. Washington, D.C.: National Education Association.

———— 1991. Cultural Difference and Cultural Deprivation. In N. Bleichrodt and P. Drenth, eds., *Contemporary Issues in Cross-Cultural Psychology*. Amsterdam: Swets & Zeitlinger.

Feuerstein, R., Klein, P., and Tannenbaum, A., eds. 1991. *Mediated Learning Experience*. London: Freund.

Feuerstein, R., and Kozulin, A. 1995. The Bell Curve: Getting the Facts Straight. *Educational Leadership*, 52(7): 71–74.

Feuerstein, R., Rand, Y., and Hoffman, M. 1979. *Dynamic Assessment of Retarded Performers*. Baltimore, Md.: University Park Press.

Feuerstein, R., Rand, Y., Hoffman, M., and Miller, R. 1980. *Instrumental Enrichment*. Baltimore, Md.: University Park Press.

Feuerstein, R., Rand, Y., and Rynders, J. 1988. *Don't Accept Me as I Am*. New York: Plenum Press.

Fischer, R. 1990. *Teaching Children to Think*. Oxford: Basil Blackwell.

Fogarthy, R., Perkins, D., and Barell, D. 1992. *How to Teach for Transfer*. Palatine, Ill.: Skylight.

Forman, E., Minick, N., and Addison Stone, C., eds. 1993. *Contexts for Learning.* New York: Oxford University Press.

Friedman, N. 1967. *The Social Nature of Psychological Research.* New York: Basic Books.

Furth, H. 1970. *Piaget for Teachers.* Englewood Cliffs, N.J.: Prentice Hall.

Gadamer, H.-G. 1975. *Truth and Method.* New York: Continuum.

———— 1980. Religious and Poetic Speaking. In A. Olson, ed., *Myth, Symbol, and Reality.* Notre Dame, Ind.: University of Notre Dame Press.

———— 1986. Text and Interpretation. In B. Wachterhauser, ed., *Hermeneutics and Modern Philosophy.* Albany: SUNY Press.

Gallagher, J. J., and Ramey, C. T., eds. 1987. *The Malleability of Children.* Baltimore, Md.: Brooks.

Gaunt, W. 1967. *The Aesthetic Adventure.* New York: Schocken.

Gee, J. 1986. Orality and Literacy. *TESOL Quarterly, 20:* 719–746.

———— 1990. *Social Linguistics and Literacies: Ideology in Discourses.* London: Falmer Press.

Geertz, C. 1973. *The Interpretation of Cultures.* New York: Basic Books.

Goody, J. 1987. *The Interface between the Written and the Oral.* New York: Cambridge University Press.

Greenberg, K., and Kaniel, S. 1990. A Thousand Year Transition for Ethiopian Immigrants in Israel. *International Journal of Cognitive Education and Mediated Learning,* 1:137–142.

Greimas, A. 1987. Toward a Semiotics of the Natural World. In A. Greimas, *On Meaning.* Minneapolis: University of Minnesota Press.

Guthke, J. 1993. Developments in Learning Potential Assessment. In J. H. M. Hammers, K. Sijsma, and A. J. J. M. Ruijssenaars, eds., *Learning Potential Assessment,* pp. 43–68. Amsterdam: Swets & Zeitlinger.

Guthke, J., and Wingenfeld, S. 1992. The Learning Test Concept. In C. Haywood and D. Tzuriel, eds., *Interactive Assessment,* pp. 64–93. New York: Springer.

Habermas, J. 1987. *The Philosophical Discourse of Modernity.* Cambridge, Mass.: MIT Press.

Halbwachs, M. 1980. *Collective Memory.* New York: Harper & Row.

Halpern, D. 1989. *Thinking and Knowledge: Introduction to Critical Thinking.* Hillsdale, N.J.: Lawrence Erlbaum.

Hanfmann, E., and Kasanin, J. 1942. *Conceptual Thinking in Schizophrenia.* New York: NMDP.

Harrower, M. 1984. *Kurt Koffka.* Gainesville, Fla.: University Presses of Florida.

Hatano, G. 1993. Time to Merge Vygotskian and Constructivist Conceptions of Knowledge Acquisition. In A. Forman, N. Minick, and C. Addison Stone, eds., *Contexts for Learning,* pp. 153–166. New York: Oxford University Press.

Haywood, C., and Tzuriel, D., eds. 1992. *Interactive Assessment.* New York: Springer.

Hedegaard, M. 1990. The Zone of Proximal Development as a Basis for Instruction. In L. Moll, ed., *Vygotsky and Education,* pp. 349–371. New York: Cambridge University Press.

Herrnstein, R., and Murray, C. 1994. *The Bell Curve.* New York: Free Press.

Holt, R. 1972. Freud's Mechanistic and Humanistic Images of Man. In R. Holt and E. Peterfreund, eds., *Psychoanalysis and Contemporary Science.* New York: Macmillan, 1972.

Holzman, P. 1976. Theoretical Models and the Treatment of Schizophrenia. In M. Gill and P. Holzman, eds., *Psychology vs. Metapsychology,* pp. 134–157. New York: International Universities Press.

Horowitz, F. D., ed. 1989. *Children and Their Development.* Special issue of *American Psychologist,* 44: 95–445.

Inbal, A. 1985. Difficulties in Diagnosing Learning Abilities in Ethiopian Immigrants and Attempts to Overcome Them. Paper presented at the Conference on Counseling in Academic Study and Vocational Guidance to Ethiopian Immigrants. Hebrew University, Jerusalem.

Kaganskaja, M., and Bar-Sella, Z. 1984. *Master Gambs i Margarita.* Tel-Aviv: Milev.

Kaniel, S., Tzuriel, D., Feuerstein, R., Ben Schachar, N., and Eitan, T. 1991. Dynamic Assessment: Learning and Transfer Abilities of Ethiopiean Immigrants in Israel. In R. Feuerstein, P. Klein, and A. Tannenbaum, eds., *Mediated Learning Experience,* pp. 179–209. London: Freund.

Kaplan, S., and Rosen, H. 1995. Ethiopian Jews in Israel. In *American Jewish Yearbook—1994,* pp. 59–109. New York: American Jewish Society.

Karpov, Y. 1995. Vygotsky as the Founder of a New Approach to Instruction. *School Psychology International,* 16(2): 131–142.

Karpov, Y., and Bransford, J. 1995. Vygotsky and the Doctrine of Empirical and Theoretical Learning. *Educational Psychologist,* 30: 61–66.

Keane, K. J., Tannenbaum, A., and Kraft, G. 1992. Cognitive Competence: Reality and Potential in the Deaf. In C. Haywood and D. Tzuriel, eds., *Interactive Assessment,* pp. 300–316. New York: Springer.

Klein, P., Weider, S., and Greenspan, S. 1987. A Theoretical Overview and Empirical Study of MLE: Prediction of Preschool Performance from Mother-Infant Interaction Patterns. *Infant Mental Health Journal,* 8: 110–129.

Koch, S. 1981. The Nature and Limits of Psychological Knowledge. *American Psychologist,* 36: 257–269.

Kojeve, A. 1986. *An Introduction to the Reading of Hegel.* Ithaca, N.Y.: Cornell University Press.

Kozulin, A. 1978. Structural and Developmental Paradigms in Theories of Behavior and Mind. Ph.D. thesis. Psychological Institute, Moscow.

—— 1984. *Psychology in Utopia.* Cambridge, Mass.: MIT Press.

—— 1986. The Concept of Activity in Soviet Psychology. *American Psychologist*, 41: 264–274.

—— 1990a. *Vygotsky's Psychology.* Cambridge, Mass.: Harvard University Press.

—— 1990b. Thinking and Speech. *Applied Psycholinguistics*, 11: 123–127.

—— 1991. Life as Authoring: A Humanistic Tradition in Russian Psychology. *New Ideas in Psychology*, 9: 335–351.

—— 1993. Literature as a Psychological Tool. *Educational Psychologist*, 28: 253–264.

—— 1994. Cognitive Revolution in Learning: Piaget and Vygotsky. In J. Mangieri and C. Collins Block, eds., *Creating Powerful Thinking in Teachers and Students*, pp. 269–287. Fort Worth, Tex.: Harcourt Brace.

Kozulin, A., and Lurie, L. 1994. Psychological Tools and Mediated Learning: Cross-Cultural Aspects. Paper presented at the Twelfth Congress of Cross-Cultural Psychology. Pamplona, Spain.

—— 1997. Graphic-symbolic organizers. Tel Aviv. Manuscript.

Kozulin, A., Lurie, L., Semionova, A., Venger, A., and Venger, N. 1995. Inducing cognitive change in adolescent immigrants from Ethiopia. Paper presented at the Second Conference of the European Association of Mediated Learning and Cognitive Modifiability. Madrid.

Kozulin, A., and Venger, A. 1993. Psychological and Learning Problems in Children Immigrants from Russia. *Journal of Jewish Communal Services*, 70: 64–72.

Kristeva, J. 1986. *Kristeva's Reader.* New York: Columbia University Press.

Kundera, M. 1995. *Testaments Betrayed.* London: Faber and Faber.

Lemon, L., and Reis, M. 1965. *Russian Formalist Criticism.* Lincoln: University of Nebraska Press.

Leontiev, A. N. 1978. *Activity, Consciousness, Personality.* Englewood Cliffs, N.J.: Prentice Hall.

—— 1981. The Problem of Activity in Psychology. In J. Wertsch, ed., *The Concept of Activity in Soviet Psychology*, pp. 37–71. Armonk, N.Y.: Sharpe.

—— [1935] 1983. Ovladenie Uchaschimisia Nauchnymi Poniatiiami kak Problema Pedagogicheskoi Psikhologii (The Acquisition of Scientific Concepts as an Educational Psychological Problem). In A. Leontiev, *Izbrannye Psikhologicheskie Proizvedeniia* (Collected Psychological Papers), vol. 1, pp. 324–347. Moscow: Pedagogika.

Leontiev, A. N., and Luria, A. 1956. Psikhologicheskie Vozzreniia Vygotskogo (Vygotsky's Views on Psychology). In L. S. Vygotsky, *Izbrannye Psik-*

*hologicheskie Issledovaniia* (Selected Psychological Investigations). Moscow: Academy of Pedagogical Sciences.

Lidz, C., ed. 1987a. *Dynamic Assessment.* New York: Guilford Press.

Lidz, C. 1987b. Historical Perspectives. In C. Lidz, ed., *Dynamic Assessment,* pp. 3–34. New York: Guilford Press.

———— 1995. Dynamic Assessment and the Legacy of L. S. Vygotsky. *School Psychology International,* 16: 143–153.

Lipman, M. 1985. Thinking Skills Fostered by Philosophy for Children. In J. Segal, S. Chapman, and R. Glaser, eds., *Thinking and Learning Skills: Relating Instruction to Research,* pp. 83–108. Hillsdale, N.J.: Lawrence Erlbaum Associates.

Lipman, M., Sharp, A. M., and Oscanyan, F. 1980. *Philosophy in the Classroom.* Philadelphia: Temple University Press.

Lompscher, J. 1984. Formation of Learning Activity. In E. Bol, J. P. P. Haenan, and M. A. Walters, eds., *Education for Cognitive Development,* pp. 21–37. The Hague: SVO.

Luria, A. 1960. *The Role of Speech in Regulation of Normal and Abnormal Behavior.* New York: Pergamon.

———— 1976. *Cognitive Development.* Cambridge, Mass.: Harvard University Press.

———— 1979. *The Making of Mind.* Cambridge, Mass.: Harvard University Press.

McLane, J. B. 1990. Writing as a Social Process. In L. Moll, ed., *Vygotsky and Education,* pp. 304–318. New York: Cambridge University Press.

Mandelstam, O. 1973. *Complete Poetry of O. E. Mandelstam.* Trans. Burton Raffel and Alla Burago. Albany: SUNY Press.

———— 1979. *Complete Critical Prose and Letters.* Ann Arbor, Mich.: Ardis.

Mead, G. H. 1974. *Mind, Self, and Society.* Chicago: University of Chicago Press.

Minick, N. 1987. Implications of Vygotsky's Theories for Dynamic Assessment. In C. Lidz, ed., *Dynamic Assessment,* pp. 116–140. New York: Guilford Press.

Modgil, S., Modgil, M., and Brown, G., eds. 1983. *Jean Piaget: An Interdisciplinary Critique.* London: Routlege and Kegan Paul.

Moll, L., ed. 1990. *Vygotsky and Education.* New York: Cambridge University Press.

Mueller-Volmer, K., ed. 1985. *The Hermeneutic Reader.* New York: Continuum.

Narasimhan, R. 1991. Literacy: Its Characterization and Implications. In D. Olson and N. Torrance, eds., *Literacy and Orality,* pp. 177–197. New York: Cambridge University Press.

Natoli, J., and Rusch, F. 1984. *Psycho-criticism.* London: Greenwood Press.

Newman, D., Griffin, P., and Cole, M. 1989. *The Construction Zone.* New York: Cambridge University Press.

Nystrand, M. 1986. *The Structure of Written Communication.* New York: Academic Press.

Olson, D. 1977. From Utterance to Text. *Harvard Educational Review,* 47: 257–281.

——— 1989. Text and Talk. *Contemporary Psychology,* 34: 119–121.

——— 1991. Literacy and Objectivity. In D. Olson and N. Torrance, eds., *Literacy and Orality,* pp. 149–164. New York: Cambridge University Press.

——— 1994. *World on Paper.* New York: Cambridge University Press.

Olson, D., and Torrance, N., eds. 1991. *Literacy and Orality.* New York: Cambridge University Press.

Omokhodion, J. O. 1989. Classroom Observed: The Hidden Curriculum in Lagos, Nigeria. *International Journal of Educational Development,* 9: 99–110.

Panofsky, C. P., John-Steiner, V., and Blackwell, P. J. 1990. The Development of Scientific Concepts and Discourse. In L. Moll, ed., *Vygotsky and Education,* pp. 251–267. New York: Cambridge University Press.

Piaget, J. 1959. *The Thought and Language of the Child.* London: Routledge & Kegan Paul.

——— 1969. *Psychology of Intelligence.* Totowa, N.J.: Littlefield, Adams & Co.

Piaget, J., and Inhelder, B. 1967. *The Child's Conception of Space.* New York: Norton.

Piaget, J., Inhelder, B., and Szeminska, A. 1981. *The Child's Conception of Geometry.* New York: Basic Books.

Polkinghorne, D. 1988. *Narrative Knowing and the Human Sciences.* Albany: SUNY Press.

Presseisen, B. 1987. *Thinking Skills throughout the Curriculum.* Bloomington, Ind.: Pi Lambda Theta.

Proffer, E. 1984. *Bulgakov: Life and Work.* Ann Arbor, Mich.: Ardis.

Raven, J. C. 1960. *Standard Progressive Matrices.* London: H. K. Lewis.

Rogoff, B. 1990. *Apprenticeship in Thinking.* New York: Oxford University Press.

Rogoff, B., and J. Wertsch, eds. 1984. *Children's Learning in the Zone of Proximal Development.* San Francisco: Jossey Bass.

Rosemarine, S., Kozulin, A., Venger, N., and Lurie, L. 1993. Modifiability of Analytic Perception as a Function of Mediated Learning. Poster presentation at the Fourth Meeting of the International Society of Cognitive Education, Tiberias, Israel.

Rosen, H. 1989. Getting to Know the Ethiopian Jews in Israel by Means of Their Proverbs. *Social Science Information,* 28(1): 145–159.

——— 1995. Working as a Government Anthropologist among the Ethiopian Jews in Israel. *Israel Social Science Research,* 10(2): 55–68.

——— 1996. Personal communication.

Rubtsov, V. 1991. *Learning in Children: Organization and Development of Collaborative Actions.* New York: Nova Science Publishers.

Rushdie, S. 1989. *The Satanic Verses.* London: Vintage.

Sakharov, L. 1994. Methods for Investigating Concepts. In R. Van der Veer and J. Valsiner, eds., *The Vygotsky Reader,* pp. 73–98. Oxford: Basil Blackwell.

Sarason, S. 1981. *Psychology Misdirected*. New York: Free Press.

Sarbin, T. R. 1986. *Narrative Psychology*. New York: Praeger.

Savell, J. M., Twohig, P. T., and Rachford, D. L. 1986. Empirical Status of Feuerstein's IE Technique as a Method of Teaching Thinking Skills. *Review of Educational Research*, 56: 381–409.

Schedrovitsky, G. 1982. The Mozart of Psychology: An Imaginary Exchange of Views. In K. Levitin, ed., *One Is Not Born a Personality*, pp. 59–63. Moscow: Progress.

Serpell, R. 1993. *The Significance of Schooling*. New York: Cambridge University Press.

Sewell, T. W., and Price, V. D. 1991. MLE: Implications for Achievement Motivation and Cognitive Performance in Low Socioeconomic and Minority Children. In R. Feuerstein, P. Klein, and A. Tennenbaum, eds., *Mediated Learning Experience*, pp. 295–314. London: Freund.

Shayer, M., and Adey, P. S. 1981. *Toward a Science of Science Teaching*. London: Heinemann.

Shif, J. 1935. *Razvitie Nauchnyh Poniatii u Shkolnika* (Development of Scientific Concepts in a Schoolchild). Moscow: Sotzekgiz.

Silberman, C. 1970. *Crisis in the Classroom*. New York: Random House.

Silverman, H., and Waksman, M. 1992. Assessing the Learning Potential of Penitentiary Inmates. In C. Haywood and D. Tzuriel, eds., *Interactive Assessment*, pp. 356–374. New York: Springer.

Silvestrov, V. V. 1989. *Filosofskoe Obosnovanie Teorii i Istorii, Kultury* (Philosophical Foundations of the Theory and History of Culture). Moscow: VZPI.

Skuy, M., Mentis, M., Durbach, F., Cockcroft, K., Fridjohn, P. and Mentis, M. 1995. Crosscultural Comparison of Effects of IE on Children in a South African Mining Town. *School Psychology International*, 16(3): 265–282.

Skuy, M., Mentis, M., Nkwe, I., and Arnott, A. 1994. Combining Instrumental Enrichment and Creativity/Socioemotional Development for Disadvantaged Gifted Adolescents in Soweto. In M. Ben-Hur, ed., *On Feuerstein's Instrumental Enrichment*, pp. 161–190. Palatine, Ill.: IRI/Skylight.

Smith, J. A., Harre, R., and Langenhove, L. V., eds. 1995. *Rethinking Psychology*. London: Sage.

Stigler, J. W., and Perry, M. 1990. Mathematics Learning in Japanese, Chinese, and American Classrooms. In J. W. Stigler, R. Schweder, and G. Herdt, eds., *Cultural Psychology*, pp. 328–356. New York: Cambridge University Press.

Stigler, J. W., Shweder, R., and Herdt, G., eds. 1990. *Cultural Psychology: Essays on Comparative Human Development*. New York: Cambridge University Press.

Strauss, S. 1993. Teachers' Pedagogical Content Knowledge about Children's Minds and Learning. *Educational Psychologist*, 28: 279–290.

Sullivan, E. 1967. Piaget and School Curriculum. OISE *Bulletin*, 2: 1–38.

Sulloway, F. 1979. *Freud: Biologist of the Mind*. New York: Basic Books.

Swartz, R., and Perkins, D. N. 1990. *Teaching Thinking: Issues and Approaches*. Pacific Grove, Calif.: Midwest Publications.

Tudge, J. 1990. Vygotsky, the ZPD, and Peer Collaboration. In L. Moll, ed., *Vygotsky and Education*, pp. 155–174. New York: Cambridge University Press.

Tulviste, P. 1979. On the Origins of Theoretical Syllogistic Reasoning in Culture and the Child. *Newsletter of the Laboratory of Comparative Human Cognition*, 1: 73–80.

———— 1991. *Cultural-historical Development of Verbal Thinking*. New York: Nova Science Publishers.

Tylor, E. B. 1871. *Primitive Culture*. London: Murrey.

Tzuriel, D., and Feuerstein, R. 1992. Dynamic Group Assessment for Prescriptive Teaching. In C. Haywood and D. Tzuriel, eds., *Interactive Assessment*, pp. 187–207. New York: Springer.

Valdes, G., and Figueroa, R. 1994. *Bilingualism and Testing*. Norwood, N.J.: Ablex.

Valsiner, J., and Van der Veer, R. 1988. On the Social Nature of Human Cognition: An Analysis of Shared Intellectual Roots of G. H. Mead and L. Vygotsky. *Journal for the Theory of Social Behavior*, 18(1): 117–136.

Van der Veer, R., and Valsiner, J. 1991. *Understanding Vygotsky*. Oxford: Basil Blackwell.

———— 1993. The Encoding of Distance: The Concept of ZPD and Its Interpretations. In R. Cocking and A. Renniger, eds., *The Development and Meaning of Psychological Distance*, pp. 35–62. Hillsdale, N.J.: Lawrence Erlbaum.

Van der Veer, R., and Valsiner, J., eds. 1994. *The Vygotsky Reader*. Oxford: Basil Blackwell.

Vosniadou, S., ed. 1994. Conceptual Change in the Physical Sciences. *Learning and Instruction* (special issue), 4(1): 1–121.

Vygotsky, L. 1978. *Mind in Society*. Cambridge, Mass.: Harvard University Press.

———— [1925] 1979. Consciousness as a Problem of Psychology of Behavior. *Soviet Psychology*, 17: 5–35.

———— 1981. Instrumental Method in Psychology. In J. Wertsch, ed., *The Concept of Activity in Soviet Psychology*, pp. 134–143. Armonk, N.Y.: Sharpe.

———— [1926] 1982. Istoricheskii Smysl Psikhologicheskogo Krizisa (Historical Meaning of the Crisis in Psychology). In *Collected Papers*, vol. 1. Moscow: Pedagogika.

———— 1982–1984. *Sobranie Sochinenii* (Collected Works), vols. 1–6. Moscow: Pedagogika.

———— [1934] 1986. *Thought and Language*. Rev. ed. Cambridge, Mass.: MIT Press.

———— 1987. *Problems of General Psychology*. New York: Plenum.

———— 1994. The Methods of Reflexological and Psychological Investigation. In R. Van der Veer and J. Valsiner, eds., *The Vygotsky Reader*, pp. 27–45. Oxford: Blackwell.

Vygotsky, L., and Luria, A. [1930] 1993. *Studies on the History of Behavior*. Hillsdale, N.J.: Lawrence Erlbaum Associates.

———— 1994. Tool and Symbol in Child Development. In R. Van der Veer and J. Valsiner, eds., *The Vygotsky Reader*, pp. 99–174. Oxford: Basil Blackwell.

Wadsworth, B. 1978. *Piaget for the Classroom Teacher*. New York: Longman.

Wagaw, T. G. 1993. *For Our Soul: Ethiopian Jews in Israel*. Detroit, Mich.: Wayne State University Press.

Wallace, B., Pandaram, S., and Modiroa, T. 1996. *Language in My World*. Kenvyn, S.A.: Juta Publishers.

Watson, J. B. 1970. *Behaviorism*. New York: Norton.

Werner, H. 1965. *Comparative Psychology of Mental Development*. New York: Science Editions.

Werner, H., and Kaplan, E. 1950. The Acquisition of Word Meanings: A Developmental Study. *Monographs of the Society for Research in Child Development*, vol. 15, no. 1.

Werner, H., and Kaplan, B. 1963. *Symbol Formation*. New York: Wiley.

Wertsch, J., ed. 1981. *The Concept of Activity in Soviet Psychology*. Armonk, N.Y.: Sharpe.

Wertsch, J. 1985a. *L. S. Vygotsky and the Social Formation of Mind*. Cambridge, Mass.: Harvard University Press.

Wertsch, J., ed. 1985b. *Consciousness, Communication, and Cognition*. New York: Cambridge University Press.

Wertsch, J. 1991. *Voices of the Mind*. Cambridge, Mass.: Harvard University Press.

Wertsch, J., Tulviste, P., and Hagstrom, F. 1993. A Sociocultural Approach to Agency. In A. Forman, N. Minick, and C. Addison Stone, eds., *Contexts for Learning*, pp. 336–356. New York: Oxford University Press.

Wickens, D. 1973. Piagetian Theory as a Model for Open System Education. In M. Schwebel and J. Raph, eds., *Piaget in the Classroom*, pp. 179–198. New York: Basic Books.

Wundt, W. 1910. *Volkerpsychologie*. Leipzig: Engellman.

Youth Aliyah. 1995. *Absorption of Young Immigrants from Ethiopia in Youth Aliyah, 1985–1995*. Jerusalem: Department of Youth Aliyah.

Zinchenko, P. [1939] 1984. The Problem of Involuntary Memory. *Soviet Psychology*, 22(2): 55–111.

Zivin, G., ed. 1979. *Development of Self-Regulation through Private Speech*. New York: Wiley.

# Acknowledgments

The assistance and inspiration provided by my colleagues at the International Center for the Enhancement of Learning Potential, founded and directed by Professor Reuven Feuerstein, are gratefully acknowledged.

Material from the following sources is used by permission: A. Kozulin, "The Concept of Activity in Soviet Psychology," *American Psychologist,* 41 (1986): 264–274, © American Psychological Association; A. Kozulin, "The Cognitive Revolution in Learning," in J. Magnieri and C. Collins Block, eds., *Creating Powerful Thinking in Teachers and Students,* pp. 269–287 (Fort Worth, Tex.: Harcourt Brace College Publishers, 1994), © Holt Rinehart and Winston; A. Kozulin and B. Presseisen, "Mediated Learning Experience and Psychological Tools," *Educational Psychologist,* 30 (1995): 67–76, © Lawrence Erlbaum Associates; A. Kozulin, "A Literary Model for Psychology," in D. Hicks, ed., *Discourse, Learning, and Schooling,* pp. 145–164 (New York: Cambridge University Press, 1996), © Cambridge University Press.

The following figures are reproduced by permission: Figures 2.1–2.3 from E. Duckworth, *"The Having of Wonderful Ideas" and Other Essays on Teaching and Learning* (New York: Teachers College Press, © 1987 by Teachers College, Columbia University. All rights reserved.), pp. 88, 91 (Figures 7.1, 7.2, and 7.7); Figures 4.1, 4.3, and 4.4 from R. Feuerstein, *Instrumental Enrichment* (Arlington Heights, Ill.: IRI/SkyLight, 1996), © R. Feuerstein, HWCRI.

# Index